Dick Bakken

The Whiskey Epiphanies

Selected Poems 1963–2013

The Whiskey Epiphanies

Selected Poems 1963–2013

DICK BAKKEN

Pleasure Boat Studio: A Literary Press
New York

First Edition

ISBN 978-0-012887-07-4
LCCN 2014933012

First U.S. Printing

Design by Susan Ramundo
Cover by Lauren Grosskopf, from a drawing by the author

Our books are available through your favorite bookstore and through **SPD (Small Press Distribution)**, **Partners/West, Baker & Taylor, Ingram, Brodart, Amazon.com,** and **bn.com**.

and also through our website via credit card:
PLEASURE BOAT STUDIO: A LITERARY PRESS
www.pleasureboatstudio.com
201 West 89th Street
New York, NY 10024

ACKNOWLEDGMENTS

"A Vision of Death" front cover sketch by DB 1/2/65, *Message of the Muse,* #6, © 2006, p. 52.

Some of these poems, sometimes in earlier versions, were published in the following periodicals and anthologies:

Abraxas Twelfth Anniversary Issue, Arizona Commission on the Arts *Artists Roster 2000–2002,* Artists in Education / Arizona Commission on the Arts / *Writer, Artspace: Southwestern Contemporary Arts Quarterly, Bisbee Daily Review, Blue Mountain Review, Bumbershoot Literary Magazine, Cabin / The Monthly Newsletter of the Log Cabin Literary Center, Calapooya Collage, Central Avenue, A Collection of Shea Poetry, Deep Down Things: Poems of the Inland Pacific Northwest, Editor's Choice II: Fiction, Poetry & Art from the U.S. Small Press (1978–1983), Ergo! / The Bumbershoot Literary Magazine, Fennel Stalk, Gold Dust: A Journal of Contemporary Poetry, Ignis Fatuus Review, Ironwood,* King County (Seattle) Arts Commission *The Arts, Message of the Muse, Mirage / The Literary Magazine of Cochise College, Mississippi Mud, Mr. Cogito, Mule, Omega, Ploughshares, Poetry Flash /* A Poetry Review & Calendar for the West, "National Poetry Week 1990 / A selection of poems / from Festival participants," *Poetry USA,* "Poet's Perspective" *The Yuma Daily Sun, Prickly Pear, Rio Grande Writers Newsletter, Second Bisbee Anthology, Sierra Vista Herald, Small Farmer's Journal, Stafford's Road: An Anthology of Poems for William Stafford, The Starving Artist Times, Star-Web Paper, The Telluride Times-Journal,* "Tucson Poetry Festival / Los Cantos de Sonora" / *The Tucson Weekly,* "Tongue in Groove" / *The Tucson Weekly, University of Washington The Daily* "Matrix" literary supplement, *Willow Springs Magazine, Zone, Zygzag Poetry & Art.*

DEDICATION

This selection from 50 years is grateful acknowledgment to the love of my life, by whom I mean my Muse, the only woman who is always here so close no matter how stupid, corrupt, unfaithful, lowdown, and lost I flounder. Whether I splash tears of fear, struggle, heartbreak, prayer, victory, fool laughter, or radiant joy, she is with me as I begin to scream, rattle, or truly open. I just do the brute work, my half of a bargain—own this my throbbing heart, take what happens to it, pulse its starts she bounties so graciously, and bear down a moment, or even a decade—until I am singing.

TABLE OF CONTENTS

1. The Truth

OREGON

Whooeee! big lumberjack,
what do you do when you get home?
You jerk the fridge and gulp
a beer. Oh so big
and hungry. Slap those buns and ketchup
onto the table beside
a pair of white nurse shoes.
But what do you do
when there aren't any weenies,
when there's a napkin taped to the next cold beer?
Jesus I'm sorry Bimbo.
Me and Oscie from the dimestore
left Tuesday for where
you ain't never gonna find us.
You drop that can and scramble the bedroom,
that's what you do. She's all gone
but those two white shoes.
And sonofabitch the Buick's not out back.
God your busted head!
all that spring in lay-up grinning nutso
with the nurse. Do you roar
through the house crying
your chainsaw into doorjamb and toaster?
Do you thrust the beer above your bent hardhat, pop it
with one squeeze, and weep
O shit as suds shoot down your arm
into the longjohns?
What you do is just stand and shake
all that ketchup into her shoes, twist the radio
high as timber cracking,
then sit and hold your big curly head.
Ketchup rolls out the eyelets
down her white shoes.
Oscar with his sunglasses is so far away hugging Lois
in your gassed purple Buick.
What do you do? What do you do, Bimbo,
when the beer you wanted is there, right there
between your two big boots?

THE TRUTH

This could be a true poem. But you
won't know. Not unless
you share a duplex wall with Larry and Helen
outside Tacoma.
There. Something made up already.
Not Larry. Oh you know that
when you see him on his birthday slam balls
to Mary Schnack in her tennis shortie.
Helen doesn't want to see. In just a robe she
downs one more swallow
by the hot oven and squeezes icings onto cupcakes
for each of Larry's two-dozen years.
If that snazzy little Schnack
even squats to tie his shoe, tell me it's black
and from there
we'll guess everything. Like Larry bounces
in after dark to get his birthday smooch and a beer.
Spread in a heart across the table—
all those pretty cupcakes.
You drank my last beer he says, lobbing a pink one
into the front room where it pops under
the couch. *Too damn hot in here*, as he snatches up again.
Hanging out in that robe!—
and he pitches one by one in there
under the couch. I could say slams with his racket.
But I want Helen to bang it on her oven like
Fuck!— Fuck!— Fuck!—
Not you he grunts wrestling the robe, shoving her stripped
onto the porch, hitting the bolt. And maybe you
could be telling the rest. No headlights, nobody in the yards,
Helen tight to the door whispering *Oh god*
Larry. Please.
I'll be good. I'll be good.
And she is good. Stretched snazz-up on the spread,
Larry naked in his black
rubber shoes, leaping over coffee table
to couch. Bouncing

above twenty-four cupcakes that'll harden there five months.
If there really *is* no duplex wall, no
Mary forever, how will you say what's happening next?
He prances past the Mixmaster— buzzing!—
Helen's robe flying from
round his neck. Onto the bed. Off. Back on. Squashes
fistfuls of icing
into his face.
I'm a big birthday bee! Falls onto her.
Bounces up over a night stand—cake pans—jockstrap—and back.
Here's my stinger!
Helen really does laugh. She wants to
love him. But can't. And
that's the truth. Even if there's no one to tell
it. Maybe Larry's birthday, maybe all these things
happen different days. Or not until tomorrow. I want—
the poem. It's all there is. But you'll have to
give me the true end. Please tell it now.
I'm standing here as lost as Larry.
And I need you. I need you.
I need you.

SATURDAY TENNIS AND SONATA

What a day! The guys
all in white
showing off sunlight. Blue sky
forever. And you go up
to volley—way back—in ethereal twist . . .
down hard wrong—*Christ!* You
won't be swilling suds with the guys
tonight.

Grimace the stairs alone. Raising a glass
of choice Chablis. To some Mozart. Your old tub
ringing full. If there's truly
elixir, it just might be
this *melody.* Hot water to the neck
and ticking away
through a cracked plug. Gaze into green vines spiraling
ceiling to knees. *Your* knees. Suddenly
your vines in shimmer. Out your open casement!—
white clouds like the guys sweeping
beyond blossoms
with the wine and adagio
into sky. And it's *your* sky, *your* white clouds
going rosy over dogwood. Breathe it all
in through the opened
blooms and wall,
through mist rising up the tendrils
from your chest as your
hands float
to sleep. This really
is your sleep. God bless your sleep.

Until you wake in dark
in the empty tub. Every tick and crescendo
long silent. Night blowing in
over your legs.
—You can't sit up. Now gasp to
twist. To lift. But you

can't— can't—
Must stare naked under vines coming down. Then finally
hear the distant voices
chorusing in.

No it's not angels. Just the guys
fresh from their suds . . .
hooting
as you strain toward their clapping hands—
No, really, guys! Goddamn.
I've been waiting for you.
Goddamn! Goddamn!

BEHIND THE HILLS

behind the hills the last pink wisp of day
    glows violet for a moment
but now it's gray
    and all the black of night tumbles down about it

      hold me, baby, hold me
      baby, squeeze me tight
      rock me, baby, knock me
      your kicking feels so right

the sky has turned to black from red
    and night breathes in my face
the moon has lost her maidenhead
    for stars alone are chaste

under the sobbing willow sweep
down past our august lost orange sun
brushed with fast breath of easy screams
our fates were drawn, and twirled, and spun
    jolt me, baby, hold me
these seats squeeze cramped and cold
    baby, twist me tight
our necks must bend and legs must fold
    rock me, baby, sock me
oh! no! again I'll soar out my soul in throes
    your biting feels too right

the steering wheel cracks my back
    so necks must bend and legs must fold
yes, why's the night always so cold
    these plastic seats christ! rake us red
there'll never be a clean white bed
    whop me, baby, shock me
ohh, no hissed croaks roll us for hope

      don't stop, don't stop, don't ever stop
      stars too far above me

love me, love me, baby, baby
  hurt me how you love me

behind the hills the last pink wisp of day
   hold me, baby, choke me
 glows violet for a moment
   baby, please don't cry
but now it's gray
   flop me, baby, sock me
 and all the black of night tumbles down
    we're torture ohh! and don't know why
        about it

THE KISS

Oh to how many
landscapes do you come
back

to love, begging
Please don't . . .

But your angel isn't going to stay.

Who cares any more
that you floated all the way out
on a silver thread of gysm
and back into that shattered vehicle
—tires spinning at heaven—
both fists on the wheel, spectacles broken
from your mortal nose.
You raised a crashed head
into wonder,
pushing out, up from all
your twisted history
into the throbbing midnight stars, the breeze
of new grass, chorused with our galaxy
of insects.

Just because—arms lifted—you walked away

in the violet that halos
trees rooted to this dearest ground

won't make her stay . . .
now.

If one star
would stream down through the vault
onto your incarnate face
flaring the attic with providence,
bloom out over yard scrabbled with limbs . . .
or just a tortoise

10

claw forth from iris blaze
after all this dead solstice cold
with her

Oh you wouldn't have to plead
Angel, please . . .

Gone so unshimmered, you lie staring
into rafters and won't shut those haunted eyes.
Your lifetimes
ago . . . awakened holy in the
road—you *had* your night of grace. Oh you
were someone else
enthralled and surrounded,
not by thistle. Arms outstretched,
you could pale now forever—stripped
of electrons, ghosting
in chrysalis sheet—and not even push out
a word.
Why should you ache
for one of those midnight crickets to stop
on your tongue? or a sudden Guernsey, eyes huge
as headlights—

Over and again and over! hurled so solo on
out of gravity, fists locked
across that heart opened into night
like a charm—
from your plexus
yet visible a translucent arc
bright back down fast
to home.

This world
is true. Let her go. You have come
all the way to these fields
of sticker and hearth
for one sure
carnal surprise—

the chill
tickle of a scorpion crossing
your throat. This is
Arizona. Your bed. Your only angel
is leaving.
There will never
stream down the splendor you puckered and
prayed for. Behold all
these legs prickling
over your chin, suddenly onto
both frozen lips
—and a horrid thorn hooked into air
your nose would suck if
you could even sweat, let alone breathe
Don't go . . .

Why not just   kiss it all off?
Your heart has become
as doomed and human as your sphincter.

But you close those throbbing eyes
—feeling so nakedly what poises on the lips—

and make your mouth say

Please . . .

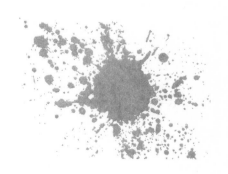

POET BEHIND THE POEM

I.

You must burn this poem, and the others,
as you would burn memories from the heart—

Take my better poem to your arms, you and
his father—bless with your double love.

Though your son has not my name, his eyes will
grow as mine until he does not understand

his tears or from whom they have come.
Never will you say his father was a poet,

but always—he is a man. Your man loves
much, giving his name to my unplanned poem

that he might have you. He who lifts my
burden, takes my respect, has my love.

II.

My children, my wife—they come for my heart
with extended palms. She knows and forgives;

they, straddling my knees, laugh into my eyes
with eyes shaped as mine—laughing as I once

must have laughed. *Promise never to see me
or the baby*—you say—*I marry in a month.*

A father's love, and a lover's—how show it—
over miles, years, silences—only in my word?

I cannot give my word, only my words. I am
happy for you and sad. Can I be indignant?

claim you? reject you? I have worked myself
into the ambiguity of my poems. There is no

longer definition—only what is. To whom
do I belong? O lovers and sons, my family!

III.

As always, I step from my life to live
in my poems. Is it sin to stalk dreams

and memories, or souls, and lech from them
these few words? Have I the right to shape

our lives? Was I wrong to make you grow?
For I have shaped you, as I shaped her,

and you will shape him also to my vision—
because his eyes are mine. You may never

burn the poem growing inside you. You are
my poem, and in you is my poem. That must

be my only claim and comfort: where I
have known and shaped the poem is mine.

IV.

So you would not belong to a poet—because
I see through words to the heart, would make

them one, shape and reshape you to my vision
—because speaking and speaking, I do not act,

only blame in riddles, step between you and
yours, comb wind and moonlight from your hair.

And you say —*because your son and pregnant wife* . . .
No, love, with words I seduce you, with words

I blame you, with words I lose you always and
win you again and lose you forever with words.

V.

Though you burn my poems to dust for the wind,
you will have always that speaking part of me—

to make you hate, and make you love. And I
will wonder always as I write: Did we love

that I might write? Do I write because
we loved? Did we love as I have written?

VI.

Would you plead that he never know
the truth in a poem? Would you save him

sadness by keeping him in the garden?
Oh, we have known, and always our poem

has been   *You, my love—the moment.*
Love, look at us now—a moment's bliss.

We can no longer live in that moment,
knowing moments twist consequences,

and now we possess them as surely as we
possess our past. How measure the worth?

Is it inevitable that he and my wife
should accept in a moment the burdens

of our moment's abandon? A new life—
a new death—can a paradox be a path?

VII.

Let my burning words bless.

Stand as you have stood, kneel
as they have kneeled, give and accept
as I have written—love as you must.

The poem is for you and for us, for him,
for one who reads, one who does not,
for my family, and for my family.

CUSTOMER OBJECTS TO NECK

See the front page lead, The Dillon Herald,
Dillon, South Carolina, November 18, 1976.

Sheriff Roy J. Lee
and fourteen deputies with dogs
surrounded a motel early this morning
to trap Willie Rogers, 43,
wanted for a crime spree last week here in Dillon.
They surprised
a man with the same name
inside frying green tomatoes and chilies, the wrong Willie
Rogers.

The spree started late Wednesday
in Pete Wallace's store when a Willie Rogers
in bib overalls
ordered Mexican beers, then a sandwich.
Wallace, as is his custom, split a chicken breast,
left the neck on one side
and served the side with the neck.
The man became incensed, jerked a .22 pistol
out of his overalls
and shot Wallace, Mrs. Wallace, and Stella Mae Dunnquist,
who was in the store trying on
a sun visor.

He ran away into the nearby gulch
as customers carried the victims to safety . . .
but under storm clouds
crept back
after sundown, broke in through a side window, stole a case
of beer and strings of sausages,
smashed cans of stove oil against the lunch counter
and lit it on fire.

With everyone scrambling
to save the store, this enraged Willie Rogers

carried flames
across to Wallace's home and hurled them in—and then their
old tomcat. As curtains flashed
Sheriff Lee, two deputies, and Jamie Wallace screaming
"Dynamite in the tool shed!" charged
to the smoking house
and in the darkness wrestled down a man
who turned out to be a bystander. Then all saw
through billows a
flamelit figure draped in sausages escape under black clouds
into the gulch with the case of beer,
yelling back an obscenity about
chicken necks.

Sheriff Lee radioed for bloodhounds
and state agents tore out of headquarters, headlights
bouncing.
When they finally came sliding
into Wallace's yard, Roy Lee pulled open a door
and all those hounds
knocked him down howling after
the poor old tom. Cat and hounds and then deputies
chased through the smoldering embers of home and store
before leashes
could be snapped on. By then
falling midnight rain
had obliterated the scent of Willie Rogers.

After the two-day downpour
Sheriff Lee was told a man in overalls
had been spotted
leaving a barn near the gulch. Lee and his deputies
found beer cans, sausage skin, obscenities and
threats on the wall,
and three sticks of dynamite.
Bloodhounds dragging leashes yowled through the gulch
but each trail brought them back around to
the barn strewn with sausage skins.
In the meantime,

two squad cars and a chicken coop were
blown up.

Then this morning Lee
and his deputies and dogs surrounded a motel
on the outskirts of Dillon and jumped
and clubbed an innocent Willie _R._ Rogers, a tire salesman
just frying up some breakfast.

Says Sheriff Roy J. Lee,
"The Willie
we want, he's somewhere in the gulch with dynamite
all right, and run out of sausages. I'm gonna round up
that nut and stick him
where he'll *wish*
he had nothing but a chicken neck to
chew on."

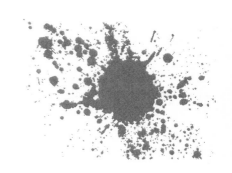

LAST WILL & TESTAMENT

I, Dick Bakken, being of sound

mind and body

—while yet pulsed with the humors, while lurching
here below our cloudflow—

by this testament yelled out behind the plow
September 20, 1867,
pass on my earthly leavings:

* * *

I leave my body—brain, heart, and belly—
rolled naked in bed sheet, cold as stopped blood

—this soggy man-tool—

to the beasts turning the sod, to beetles and bores,
any who'll nuzzle
me then.

May every kissed grit of my flesh
and spirit
slime through a worm's bowels
to jelly the tilth
with the sweet smell of
mold.

Dump this silly meat in a ditch, good fellow, and be glad
I was born.

* * *

I leave my name

to my children—cracking these reins all bejesus—

and my velocity in their
veins.

Any what's-his-hey will hustle
behind his plow
and catcall, hoot through the weather, fall
on a woman and groan for
his sons,

little men stepping
beside him
with names like quail cries and whinnies.

His little girl
will learn to sigh and whore holy
as a fieldful of us. O bless

this quick flesh, headlong under thunder

down into weeds and sheet. With luck she'll ditch
his name
for a beast of a man, all giddy up
and whistle and a heart
like the rain.

* * *

I leave my children, Eric and Creseyde—blushing

with blood, in their angelic
falls of hair, shy and sliding away
as eels—

to the world and its fare—to skunk snuff and magpies—

as every child
under this sky is left, all our darlings,
each to a turn in the sod.

May they bloom
dewy as morning glory
till the sun
shines them shut.

* * *

I leave my wife, Pamela—delicious

spirit!—

to her lovers and swine. Let a legion lick and hump
her till she tumbles plumed
or splits,
then maggots naked in her eye pits and ass
screw her giddy.

O give her everything she loves!

* * *

I leave my wenches and hussies

cheery and glistened
as worms, who slide me down witless, our blissed lips
hissing *Sweet!*—

to my good fellow, all steamed in linen and this
electric breeze, jerking his jesus
crazy with sweat and
spittle.

Now our dead mamas
and their poor dead priests can't
swoon
that our meat makes us kiss

till come to the finish
with bishop and bedfellow, dumped in a ditch-end, we humor
the worms:

Yes, nuzzled together,
my horse and the landlords, all our mums
kissed brainless,
turned over with the sweethearts
and dirt.

* * *

I leave my poems with *Geehaw!* and *Hey!*, *Whoop!*
and *Whoa!*

in the wind

with all my breath and whistle.

These poems and hollers, flash and thunder crack
will not gee up
the dead
nor call back their sneeze and sass.

Balls-up, head popped with rootlets and bugs,
I won't give a hoot
when this mouth falls apart
in the rain.

* * *

So I leave my goods.

Now, you barkers and hawkers—

spit and squall for them, bellyache, snatch
to your breasts

till kingdom come—*ha hah!*—these no-good armfuls,
not a lick of cheer to worm

or fellow.

* * *

O all in downpour

I leave my good fellow his belly for
humping and so many bright

worms.

24

2. Bloodline

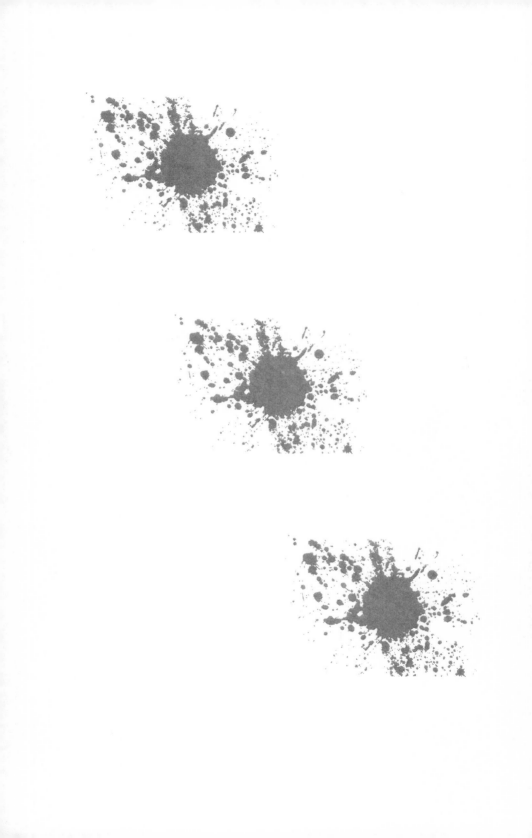

THE RUBY

i don't know what happened today
lunch while tipping a swallow of milk
chill and rich
suddenly i was back on the ruby
a boy of seven again with my grandfather
barefoot in cool sand
my pole plunging the misted sunlight
don't give him slack my grandfather whisped
you keep that line tight son
my thumb already burnt raw by the whining reel
arms spent from levering the long pole high
grandpa grandpa he took the worm
i cried when my rainbow burst into sky
twisting and glistening
silver-flashed through leaps of spray
pull son keep it tight no slack
my arms how they ached with joy
i've got to keep it tight grandpa i mustn't give him slack
look how he shines oh there he goes
i can't hold him grandpa i can't hold him
hold him son
and i held him until he rose into sparkles forever
still dodging fiercely back and forth
coax him in son
easy
pull and reel pull and reel in the mist-prismed dazzle
see how he swims in circles grandpa see i've got him now
not yet son careful
ooohhhhh!
the reel whined into my flaring thumb
grandpa grandpa
ease him in again son
my arms pull and reel pull and reel oh my arms
grandpa the net the net
he's too big for the net son
he was too big for the net he shimmered so
grandpa he's too big for the net
and i curled one hand on the line as grandfather had taught

keep the line tight hold your pole high
i held that pole high and slid down the leader
into my rainbow's gasp
hooking his gills with my fingers i hoisted him out
flipping and twisting shining splashing sand and water
i wrestled up over that shore with him
droplets flying high
heaved him flashing into green
grandpa see him i got him i got him
my grandfather was lifting our thermos from the river
he spun that red cap off and stretched me the streamed bottle
while my rainbow flopped down dewy grass
yes he's a big one he said as i tipped the thermos
with aching arm
to gulp such chill milk

HOW TO EAT CORN

My grandfather ate squash, ate corn. He ate corn
like this, lifting the ear, saying
You eat corn like this, when you eat corn
eat like this. And I pulled shuck and silk away
and saw the worm. On and on
as Grandfather lifted ears and spoke and showed
his teeth and the yellow sun passed again and again,
the worm was curled under my thumb
only a shuck-width away, saying
This is how I eat corn. Like this. Like this.
I eat corn like this. When I eat like this
I am eating corn.

BLOODLINE

No matter skin and kiss, no
matter cries of love. All
all all is
falling away, even mama and babe.
Family and love but illusion, breasts pulsing
a same blood, all
that whistling long distance.
Yet a never seen
nor lifted grandchild says
"Bowwow"
to Papo and Nana as Mama and Dada
bend far into their other line—
Suddenly space opens
its one vast
heart holding
us all.

WEDDING GIFT:
Four Spoons, a Jar of Honey, Dried Rosehips

You are Sally, Bride, and Aunt.
Sister, you will be Mother.

1
These silver spoons
were a wedding gift from our Aunt
Alva,
five times a bride,
who drank like a fish, flopped
with her men, and woke up
dead in bed alone
in her mountain cabin.

In Alva's sheets
I kissed my bride from ears to toes
and breathed all night
faster than the river was sliding
by
while she sighed
Help me.

We woke marveling
to be groom and bride, flesh
tart with brine,
bodies
dappled new with blood, smelling
of milt and roe.
We slipped together
and did not think to fathom
our dream:

Alva, dizzy as a lord,
rolled in her billowing lace
and did not hear
the river rushing away.

She hung on to each thrashing groom
and cried
Sweet, I am dying.

2
You are named Sally for me
after the first
girl I loved, but Pamela
sallied me sweeter and slicker than any—
O quick as a fish I was quivering
and done.

Cockcrow and cockcrow,
hips bright on the briers, I woke
to kiss
her shining belly. We rose
to pump and fire
our bath and the tea
and splashed with the sucklings
who made you aunt.

When Alva breathed, men
started alive, apples fell to the ground.
She whirled and maple leaves slid
away on the water.
We loved our bodies rising
from her bed and kept our sap
warm,
stirred honey in tea with these
spoons, now yours.

Drinking while the river went
shallow—under slipping cedar shakes
in our hands
hips fell apart in the teacups,
like the cabin and everything else,
leaving dregs to mull
and dream:

Alva—lord! juiced to the gills! —
raising
her cup to good health.
She tossed off groom after groom
and roared, swigged
her applejack and merry and cockeyed
stumbled to bed too stiff
to get up.

I sat up cold in Alva's sheets
with drafts rolling the curtain lace,
over and over
geese flying the river
away south.
Pamela lay waking in linen
far away as the swells that billowed
by while I unveiled
my bride.

3
All Alva's grooms though they fumble
in her sheets till sap and the river flow
back, fear they will come
to nothing
but the damp and draft.

Sally, I'm chilled stiff
by bride's lace, and curtain, sleet,
slush, ceiling, and bed
in a heap—thickets to bloom,
pheasants awake—
where her hips and Alva's
rose and rose.

The velocity in our blood, heat
in our breasts, fails
to quicken frost from the maples and ice
from the water.

We always ebb and sleep
though newly wed and drunk
as lords.

But a bride and her groom
though they cry *Help* from their bed
do not fail
to come to their death.
A bride though she die and die again
only wakes in the salty air
niece and aunt,
a bride, unlaced, wound in sheets
with her groom.

4
Bubbling Sally Lovelace
made me blush and grin when I was a boy
and you woke up
alive.
Because now
you are aunt and Sally in veils
and the river does not flow
back,

here is honey to your health
and silver spoons. You need only a cup
to fill
and raise and fill
and the dregs to tell what blooms
for a rosy wink.

Here is to Sally dressed up
in a curtain, dreaming the playhouse
bride. Here is my face
shining.

Eric is in my lap, Pamela
seeded with Creseyde.

Here is Alva walking toward us, well
water brimming in her
cup.

And here is today
in the mountains—where the cup
lies still against the cool
pump.

OPOSSUM

1
Sudden
as moonlight—
your bristles silver,
seep
dark with blood.
Your eyes
smashed open forever,
your grin fixed and beastly
curl my lip. These
hands stiffen around
such bare
thumbed feet.

In fright
here, we hunch
under broken clouds—
blaze-face or man
—grinning and fathering.
Not so dead
until we scurry across
the onflying line
from pouch to
doom.

2
Opossum . . .
in lightning
I lay these hands into
your leaking hair—
an ooze yet
warm.
The lice
that drank your heart
now drink mine.

I bear
you, primal sire,
agrasp the thick, raspy past
—swinging
in your rupture
of sleep—down into
nodding
roadside brome
as scud glimmers over.

3
Though I be
the eerie,
tailless beast crushed,
smiling into dimmed stain,
do not prod long
snouting
my frozen gaze. Sneeze
out your breath.
Hulk on into shined rain. O!
paling hands, wash
off that haunt
of face.
Wheeze alone
on a lair of corn husks—
twitch one dream:

In April
we are newly naked,
fumbling with
our first wee digits.
Dozing
on backs snuggled at nest,
open orbs rolled
weird—we glaze, grin
from sleep
as fathers in feint.

4
You rise
dumbly, lifting
large blinded luminous
eyes
toward my light
and thunder.

I swallow your dull awe
as I rush
over.
A shadow sways
behind me,
up-dazzled by
bolts.
Such blaze of face,
flashed
and helpless—
is my father.
I cling to his blousy front.
Crouching, he
falls into thicket.

5
I blink open to
the moon
and a musk of possum
on my hands, sniff
the breeze ruffling my hair.
My thin ears
tremble
in the chill.

LAST NIGHT, THIS AFTERNOON

A muscular boy breathing wine
dives off rocks into the river and splits his skull,
floats up crumpled bubbling red into
water flowing on.

I gasp into the bleeding gash,
her hot legs kicked wide on the bed. Dark blood
on my hands and cock. Cherry
wine on her lips,
on my eyelids and brow.

Cradled in my arms, moaning
sweet breath. Alive! His muscles ripple and tremble.
I gape into the deep gash
oozing wine
all through his surly hair.

Lull the helpless flesh at my breast,
rock and whisper, my dumb eyes
pulled to the wound
split ghastly between her legs.
Groaning woman! All we horrified men fall
dizzy from gore.

Where am I? What happened? Who
are you? Please hold me. Am I dreaming?
My head hurts. My head hurts. My head hurts.
I think I'm falling.
Aieeee.

Breathing wine, I glide alive back up
into the slash I fell from, my own poor darlings fall
from shrieking. Oh, there's no help, no help
but to hold flesh dear
and rock and shudder to a last
sob.

Belly-deep in the river, bleeding
through gash and hair,
she muses up at a sunlit youth—whose shadow falls
over her. Help!
His burst head dreams billowing red blooms
into water passing. Help!
Somebody help us.

Half way between head and cunt
is the heart
pumping rivers both ways.
While the heart pumps—wine streaming out, dull-blue
streaming back—head and cunt will bleed
and give birth. Aie!
and pour out into what slides
past us.

We rub the chill from our flesh,
each holding to an end of the wine-and-blue towel,
rubbing body and then face, looking
down the veined towel into eyes
of man, eyes
of woman.

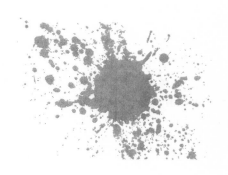

SHINING GRASSHOPPER

Kiss her with dew
who drinks here at dawn

springs up all wings

into rainbow
about the sprinkler

high how a whisper floats

down through the sky
through my knees

tlink!

into a goblet of
spring water

Sweet green cadillac

ashine on the tip
of my finger

wiping two wispy sensors

O I point
back into iridescence . . .

Mother I love

you drinking the clear
milk of my heart

WHIRR

1
And I wake in first light
beside Grandma Ethel upstairs in our big
warm bed. She *puk puks* to a chicken in bare arms
from last night's box by the pillow,
fingering mush down its weak white throat. Out of her ancient
nighty pimples dingle like soft pearls. Then all the
luscious wrinkles of her face
shine full on me.

Once so early in our
light, head out the high curtains, a last star still blazing
in heaven, I spied a Chink pheasant
prancing the front grass. Fierce tufts of spirit
burst at crown
as it stretched up, breast
thrust, whirring those iridescent wings
afire. *Step step hop* it whirled to charge the dawn with a
heart-startling cry.

Flame! Flame! My red setter
is already astride the dry manure pile in back,
alive to spot a Chink whirr down bright
out by our cow trough, scoot across the irrigation ditch.
O we'll be
away through pasture
grass into old Mansfield's whipping
corn after that thunder-up of wings for our
astonished faces. Flame dances
to me sideways, grinning all her teeth, wagging head to haunches
that I'm here.

In her kitchen
barefoot, Grandma has split
kindling, fired up the one true stove.
She guffaws bad jokes to our invigorated chicken
without her dentures, slurping batter off a hot spatula
in high wheezing laughter. She's

always in the same loose dark rayon dress flecked with light
and milk. My Flame
pushes into both hands so I can squeeze
those ears while I gape at Grandma's big knobby
bunions and hammer toes.

2
Scrub the kitchen, paint
a porch. Grandma can't stop gabbing
and working. Up a ladder she's—*flip-stroke flip-stroke*
with that brush—
talking so fast to nobody, spraying spit
onto her glasses. Flame and I
are tunneled
into pasture grass grabbing at garter snakes
when—*Boom! Cripes!*—a nest of wild chicks explodes
all over our sky. Grandma flushes the red from her fingers
and pop-out teeth under garden hose.
She's picked a tree of cherries
in a skewed visor,
set the sprinklers, kissed that chicken back into
our coop of squawking whites. Hustling again for the kitchen
in those sturdy black half-heels, Grandma's
just whispers, eggs afloat on
her apron. Flame and I
splash down an irrigation ditch. *Oh!*
you're gonna git the polio!—if she catches us
wet. *You're gonna!— You're gonna git!—* on into eternity.
But Flame points
a fanned bluegill gasping the last
puddles in a melon patch. Dashing for home
we duck low
through that empty ditch alongside old Mansfield's corn
with sticky faces and a
squeaking fish.

Past sprinklers in mist-sparkled
rayon and hairnet, apron swishing, Grandma appears

at the sunbright stump. She's got two squawkers by the legs
and her flashing hatchet.
Whack!
For once those
dumb whites thrill slick as Chinks sprinting,
squirting red high out the neck, through our sprinklers
over yard—*hoppity flop!*—and garden.
In their heart rain
Flame is fast
beside, nose low, barking them
around and back, leaping with both into a rainbow.
Grandma snatches the sky
full of feathers, kicks those twitching heads
to our jumpy cat, then huffs off toward the sparks in her stove.
Atop manure Flame is lapping splashes from her snout
and flair of a tail.
Grandma cries *Yoo-hoo!* from the porch.
Doggy boy! Find me some wild
asparagus!

Beneath a lightning-slashed
elm behind the barn I stretch past noon
on chin and arms watching grasshoppers snap down
into my gaze. The day is awhirr in emptiness. I'm wondering
where Flame is gone
loping her nose
now. From that distant
kitchen I can hear Grandma echoed
alone—scolding, stamping. She's so sure
old Mansfield is the pistol shock that ripped our
cat's ear off.
Under this emblazoned trunk
I laze round to drift
skyward—
Jeeminy Cripes! A host of Chinks
stunned over *me* upon the singed boughs! All blinding noon
suspended just above my mind, pulsing like the
stars that wait for me
unseen. I'm so close under their luminous feathers of fire.

I don't know why clustered aloft in opened daylight.
Don't know why electrified for apocalyptic
shimmer. Why blinking down into
my heart only.

3

Flame! Flame!
From up so high I can see my Flame
rolling with the yardful of kinfolk, fetching and
barking. Below through leaves
in sunlight
dazzling tablecloths
drape plywood on sawhorses
heaped with another of Grandma's last
Memorial feasts. I drop a few white feathers, wishing
them voltage. Now here she comes new in deep flowered rayon
hoisting a platter of holy corn
on the cob. I should hail
poor old Mansfield over, out flinging manure about
his dirt, before he sneezes and dies.
Come and git it!
But I'm
down my tree
like heaven's own
snake.

Apples and walnuts
shivered through a salad. Yes and gladness
with the roar of Grandma's fiery stove. Chicken resurrected
out of its flaring sauce. I cradle big jugs of grape
Kool-Aid. Here's bright shelled peas
to bounce
our bibs like the moments. Churned butter
is slipping dimensions
into hot squash.
That ascending dipper shimmered
with giblets spills into
worlds of Grandma's fluffy potatoes. Biscuits break open

for blackberry jam. Perfect asparagus
from old Mansfield's roadside
on into our future sighs. O! there's gonna be
cherry-bled ice cream
handcranked by
cousins!

Grandma bustles out
another steaming chicken. *Here's that ol' hen*
I took to bed! She guffaws solo,
talking nonstop, spraying
spots across
the tablecloth. *Well this squawker*
sure shook her wattles on the stump for my jokes! Ha! ha! ha!
Corn kernels dribble from her creamy lips. My own real
Grandma Ethel,
wheezing her face into
wrinkles, growing warts like a
garden. *Lordy! who's gonna snatch this*
fancy dress when I croak! She pops out her teeth
to lick them off,
then blusters back indoors
with a fart at each porch step, laughing so hard
in the kitchen while she whips a high cloud of cumulus
for our cobbler. We're all as happy
as Flame with a grin
full of shocked feathers.

4
O so long ago through streaked
light of day the sheriff's rippling Ford glides into
our gravel. I'm picking strawberries again with Grandma,
on fire to tell how many flops a squeaking
fish has yet.
But I have to hunch
in that smother of a ride all the way back to a ditch
beside old Mansfield's scraggly corn, step into a few wild spires
of asparagus—

and name my Flame.
Flame!

Grandma is out waiting in the gravel
anew, in all her anxious wrinkles like then—that same ancient
bright-flecked rayon—where she can catch me running
dead for home. In Grandma's
arms I'm gasping
so hard I'll never stop.
Truth
jolts the two of us
entwined. Like strychnine
convulsing one
gut. Grandma is choking for Flame, for my blown
out heart, and those last foamy squeals into manure dirt.
The world just falls away—like daylight,
feathers—
but for Grandma
and me in the burning perfection
of our clutches. Here
through the bloomed red sky
of my childhood, all Grandma's tears, her shiniest
slobbers, wash the crown of my hair, stream
my neck. The unstoppable waters of
my eyes and nose
and my resounding throat, sop Grandma's heaving bosom deep
through her ordinary dress
of stars.

It is done. Yes
this whirr of my days. At last now, Grandma.
Open your arms. Let me
step out breathless into our blossoming field of sprinted earth.
And a Chink of radiance thunders
up to burst above me. *Cripes!* I am only
the simple heart of awe
that calls

Flame! Flame! Flame! O my Flame! Grandma. My Flame

3. The Happy Birthday House

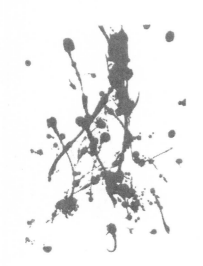

SALUD!

A free-form spring sonnet

Yes. *To us!* This hum
round two heads, two hearts ashine
at the trellised doorstep. In one
toss— our brightness that is wine.
Burning into whisper, haloed
with roses and desire, afire
on our faces, a whole blossomed
earth thrumming its wild lyre
of wings. The fragrance! the ruby-throats!
Bordeaux with sky's buzz! to last
quaff. Clash the goblets
and kiss. In flashes of chance
uplifted O! from blouses, from trousers,
we rise to bliss, like sipped flowers.

THE COMING OF SPRING

We keep it *inside,* each
deep at home—
Urgency
for more than a shower, a fresh blouse
of wet. O more
than lace over a table
in this room
hidden
among *trees of heaven.*
If I climb a chair,
shove out
the skylights and dare even your name
to the luminous buds,
your feet stop naked there
where you are.
Up green
along the puddles
between any house and
at last this other,
shoots
a bush, roots thrilled down our
odorous dark,
while everything streaks
with secret.
Open your eyes and you are here,
sending out the
perfect one bloomed rose
of your hand,
each of us *in gaze*
into the other's new face, thunder
rushed in over the hills.
Who will know
we each whisper to our blown curtains
alone
as you ascend onto
the table and here I crash
lace and goblets away to my floor.
There you whirl! hands

flashed
out through a ceiling, hips like that
wind we each hear bring in
the clouds.
It's even darker
with the fragrance of your hair
lifting the house—and *oh!*
undersilks come wisping as amorous as
rain to both floors.
These are my shrieks, my claps of
laughter
while all that lightning
cracks straight into each heart.
Who stops outside
on the stairway and sighs in a downpour
Oh sad. Poor lonely.
Thank heaven
I hear you in there in
the silver shower
flood with our sparks charging
down your thighs . . .
While under such earth-curved boughs
I whisper around
in this room
to the soaking furniture that at last
you are here, are here,
my darling, all green and so
newly slender.

SPRINKLER RAINBOW

Sally in the skyflashed
swing, red ribbon breezing
half out her muddy
hair. She's been rolling with stolen kitten
in squeals over leaky garden hose
flattening Mom's peppermint shoots. O Sister's
gonna get it when Mom flairs
out to drag the sprinkler. But a tiny green leaf
stuck to Sis's forehead
sets off that trailing scarlet
to make Sally gleam a wild leprechaun
with kitten of dirty gold
on her lap in
sweeping sunflame.

BLUES FOR WILDMAN WILLIE

Walked in the Spokane
foothills where Willie used to shack.
Someone had smeared a boulder
I hate you,
young lovers. Beware
lest you are damned
in this life and the next.
Heard an owl.
Back down on the avenue
met an old juiced wino who cried
homemade blues at me
all night.
Had my pen, jogged it all down.
Said way back '38 he jammed
with Hank Williams.
Now no guitar, but jerked up
his sleeve and fingered the chords
on his wrist pretty
as could be.

KATHLEEN'S ADVICE

I remember
after Dan came back from Vietnam
he sat around the kitchen
all spring in his jockey shorts
poking at an egg.
Finally he looked at me,
said, "I'm depressed. I want
to be married
but don't know any girls."
"Well, why don't you
get dressed up and comb that hair.
Take a brisk jaunt downtown,
see if you can
find anyone might like
to marry you." Damn! if he didn't
bounce up spiffy all Saturday
at A.J.'s Department Store grinning
"Don'cha wanna marry me?"
Then he thumbed
home and threw off his clothes
to spin like this world.
He'd laughed it
out of his system, mussed his hair,
and felt like sailing
waffles over the neighbor's
collie.

DAN'S BANANA WEDDING CAKE

He was like that.
He'd get a notion. Like
wearing his jockey shorts around the yard.
Like wanting walnuts on his wedding
cake. Like the best were hung
from that high branch.
"Don't do it! Don't do it!"
cried Shirley Mae slamming out with a
big bowl of batter.
But Dan was already up the tree in his jockeys.
So she just kept stirring and shrieked on
about risking everything—
while Dan lay way out straddling
that high limb.
He had two hands and a mouth full of nuts
before the branch cracked off
dropping him eight feet to the next branch down
—where he lit just like that.
Shirley Mae didn't know
she'd stopped shrieking, that the batter
slopped over her feet.
Well, that's no way to land—
But heaving to suck his wind back
Dan managed to almost smile,
and squeaked
"I lost my nuts."

SHIRLEY MAE HONKS THE HORN

Shirley Mae never
liked her bent wedding band
and puny ruby. So one
day when she left it on the sink
Dan hocked it
and bought some beer.
A burglar rushing through town
flashed them
a silver ring with a big topaz
and two snazzy diamonds.
Dan slapped his whole income tax return
beside the thing
while Shirley Mae slipped it on
shining.
"I want to go dancing!"
A week later she forgot it
in a roadhouse john
and cried
two days before Dan could find out why.
"Get in the VW, Shirley Mae!"
They wheeled
all over that podunk, Dan blaring
on a rented loudspeaker
"Reward! Reward!
She's lost her wedding ring!"
while Shirley Mae blew her nose
and prayed and
got aspirin stuck to
her hanky.

THE HAPPY BIRTHDAY HOUSE

I'm in love. Yes, with you.
With dough balls
in my pants, wads in the sheets, sweet gummy
dabs frolicked kitchen to closet.
O I am. It's my heart. I'm all sweet,
I'm sliding. With grape skins, dribbles, red juice
on my hands, tickled on your apron, swirled
through your new-rolled dough.

I smell of honey and brew. Marry me
a little, my fancy, my dainty, today and tomorrow.
Light up your oven. Dance,
dance me to bed
in your sticky, powdery arms.
Warm. Warm.

My *manna*!
Let me breathe-in this
whole house your oven warms.

Mmmm, your hands . . . new bread . . .
your yeasty, naked smell, my tasty, fermenting blankets
and kitchen.

Who rolls and punches the flesh-stuff?
Who squeezes arms, legs out
from the lump
and pinches noses and toes?

My breathing pretty, *you* just
steam asleep under blankets in oven air.
Somehow it works. Your busy flesh
sweats, pulses, bubbles,
and sighs. So does your dough as you drowse and swell
and mist till this house smells like the sweet
gum we're made of.

Open the closet— Oops! here I am,
whistling, patting the jugs.
Oh, into your wedding dress again! Wine works
like you giggle. Our clothes smell of this houseful,
this air. One good sniff
and I'm off, a dandy little bibber dancing
with you. Well, one two—and tra-la.
Good humor, good spirit. Whee! our own juice
to cheer us up nimble.

Quick, who tickles heart till it squirts,
makes flesh fizz and babble?
Who gives birthday
and hiccup, titter, sweet red flush
fanny to lips?

I'm a lump, a dumpling, a doughboy
dropped alive into bed. A whole house smells of woman
and bread. I'm in love, I'm loony. Marry me
some more, give me a squeeze,
fill me with wine. I'm going to make
this stuff sing.

Pounding and squashing and laughing—
What are you doing
in the kitchen in your apron? Are you pinching
little men and women? Are you patting them
to sleep in your cozy oven?

Side by side, steaming
in blankets, we blink awake. Is it
a birthday? A wedding?
Who poked me? Is it time for a kiss? Am I fresh?
Shall we dosi-do? Shall we imbibe?
Or shall we tell who makes us
puff and fancy?

Look at the little drunken man and woman!
Yes, they're alive! It's their blood makes them dizzy.

They are dancing, they are married, they love
their boozy, doughy flesh.
They don't care who gives them
O their own sweet smell!

No, take and eat, take and drink, take and marry.
We are guests, we are glad
in their house and dance in their clothes
and odors. We squeeze them, we feast,
we soil their bed.
Just look at us, pasty and juicy
to the elbows!

CANTICLE FOR HER BEDROOM

bless fluttery Jo Ellen bless
her gait her song her white hands
on her face the door bless
the room
bless bless bless
the room all the light the air bless
bless the room the dove the lilies
bless her loving gaze
now only for Bill yes o bless
her white hands dropping combs bracelets rings
white blouse white
panties lilies bless the floor
bless her hands on her lips nipples cunt
o bless her closed eyes
her love coo bless her breath
bless air bless light bless walls brilliant
lilies doilies jars earrings perfumes book-and-coins
bless bless the turtling dove entranced
white feathers afloat air light
around her bless the room
she fills with joyous breathing
white feathers floating petals panties
bless her white hands what they do
her face held oh in his hands kissed kissed kissed
yes o bless tremors come all over them bless
bless Jo Ellen bless Bill bless love
bless hair eyes hands breath
breath breath
the room
light air feathers desire disarray
bless bless bless bless
pants pulled recklessly off
spilled pennies across the feathered
flowered unregarded floor bless
her bless her bless her
bless Jo Ellen

MOWING THE GLORY WITH EUNICE
IN HER WHEEL CHAIR

Me out
rolling her around and
around the yard as she shrieks
in spits, waves a wallbanger, spattering
into dandelion
and vine. *Lord God*
the rain
really popped our spot
this morning, Har. Her swept
sparkling
glasses, her yellow turban
dotted with vodka. Clippings, petals
flown up all over us,
gnats rising
from the scattered glory. *Jesus,*
Harv, it's coming
faster than we can roll. Charging on around—
a gnat
to my brow—
there's just our
run at that last tuft of green
in the center. *Harvey,*
here's to Lord Almighty and the heart.
Fly on over. And pulling up sudden
to slap my face, I watch her
sail out
onto a new lawn.

BRAHMAS AT THE DUMP

Below these huge thunderheads
heaving in, a dozen black humpback
bulls wade our trash. They're butting
great garbage bags like balloons
into the roadway. Here they chomp
and bounce them until field clippings
burst out swirling in gusts.

Whiskers fanned from the chin,
old trash pickers hunch against this
gale. A raven blows by us
with tumbleweeds and cardboard. *Goddamn*
the pickers won't wait—and stomp
across bottles toward the bulls, metal
detectors crackling. *Hiya! Hiya!*

Yi! those bulls lurch backward
with snorts through big hot nostrils.
Shoulders humped higher than
our dusty truck, they glare in the blast
dead at us—withers jumpy, horns
white as lightning—and chaw their grass
as it skeins down onto trembled dirt.

The geezers want to feel steel
thrilling up the arm. They pound their
detectors. *It's gonna rain, you dumb
bastards!* Nacho smashes glass.
Boomer whirls electrical wire, *zwhooming*
bulls back. Donald lobs an armless
dolly up into wild static. *Hiya! Hiya!*

From off in the refuse, one
crazed bull tramples bellowing out, a
flame-haired mannequin aloft on
his horn, trailing confetti and surgical

tubes. He kicks like he'll charge
the old farts. Then lightning *ka-racks!*
and we're all banging-over barrels,

bawling, hats snatched, as the
redhead flies up naked into the storm.

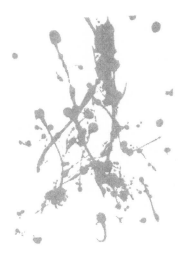

LETTER FROM DEBRA

Living in a tent
has really calmed me down.
That fear of darkness
is almost gone. Charles was away
for some nails right before full moon
—and I loved the nights
alone. I bathed in the water tank
by moonlight
and slept so naked.

Lately the foxes
are moving in closer. I glimpse
their faces through my fingers while
sipping tea. At dusk
the vixen hunts across our meadow.
When I whisper, she stops—
and shows her tongue. She and her mate
drink from the old water tank
where I bathe.

Michael comes out
from town on weekends. He never
gives me noise when I shake
off my dress and dance just because
there's a moon.
At midnight on solstice
he'll shinny whatever one glimmered oak
I step to
and steal mistletoe.

These shy little creatures
are coming so close—
They sit out in the chaparral and watch
while I'm alone in my nightgown
like I won't know
they're here. I don't want to disturb them
with hammering

or have cats or dogs. They drink
from the water I bathe in.

Charles says
our cabin is nearly finished.
But I don't want to live inside walls
any more. In the tent
I can look out at the stars, breathe
blown air. I love undressing and waiting
in the meadow tank
where my foxes
wet their naked tongues.

DEAR AUNT HELEN . . .
LOVE, JANE

Yesterday
the first of February
while circling Eagle Peak above
the San Carlos Reservation
Nelson and I
were married at 10,000 feet by wind
round an Apache pastor.
We floated
in the tail of the plane, lace
lashing our faces, while Zephie
shouted Bible verses and wedding vows
and prayed for us,
his ragged hair vertical.
So imagine a
saint with one cloudy eye,
fragrant as tobacco like your own
Rafaeldo.
I had asked him
what was he ready to
recite for our plunge into ceremony,
said we wanted to let go that
word *obey.* I told him
—nippled in your cirrus of a blouse—
I'm not really a Christian
but do believe in
something
and he asked was it okay to
say *Holy Matrimony*
and strike a light. Lord
I said *do.*
He blew a perfect
cyclone of smoke. It was glorious
up there with the sun
setting, all of us toppling, and the plane
in a slide. So much like you
this trombonist
honked up breathless

at takeoff
bolting in rose jogging togs
to vault aboard and be our witness.
She said, best
darn dream happened to her in a long time
to cry in a wedding all in the air,
that gauze snapping off me.
She invited us down
for duck dinner and when we
came sailing in
well there were only two silver places
with tall goblets, candelabras, and a surprise
toss of blossoms and rice.
She and her whispering husband
waltzed among their
shadows and just waited on us
reflected in glass in starry kimonos
until we were ready at last
for our taxi. So now off to a roar, here
with Nelson on the porch swing in sunrise—
as you always promised
I am suddenly a
swept bride,
my lips to the wind, such chill
gusts shrieked through
your whirling blouse into
my heart.

4. Just Above Any Little Town

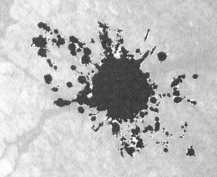

RUN

I spied
a penny. I
did not stop. A snake
hooped down an edgy road.
She cracked me
with a strap of spit. The big fist
of roses closed its ripe eye. Now puff
another slope
and smell that dead star fizzing
love at the ditch. Why
bow only to some thousand-cicada
blur? Snow blazed
my face. You saw the sun
twist seven times. Who
swallowed big pounding on the roof?
Lightning shrieked across her
other hillside. I
sobbed those dogs barking
on and on.

HIGH IN IDAHO ROCKIES*

So lost since daybreak way up
wakened in all that oxygen,
I crashed down through wild
brush to step up on log rot
suddenly breath to breath
with an elk. I knew his heat
wafting my face, eyes widened
as mine. I could have touched
his quivering lips, that heart
pounding into my chest.
Alive with oxygen I marveled
through a span of antlers revolving
with that great head and all of me
before he stepped calmly away.
I heard him vanish into brush
and silence, then down beyond
where he had breathed, a cutbank
wavered, thus a road. He dissolved
back up into Idaho, me an hour
on down into Montana and
a long hypnotic trudging out.

*Ends of evergreen needles and mist
droplets from creek cascades make
points round which oxygen is created.*

STEPTOE BUTTE

is a quartzite island jutting 3,612 feet out of
rolling Palouse lowlands, Whitman County,
Washington, a great tower over 400 million
years old looming bald grandeur above 15-7
million year Columbia River basalt beneath
the rest of the Palouse. On top, you can see
200 miles . . . for Mike and Carol Vaughan.

One

Around around our old car whined
winding up the steep spiraled road
onto summit of Steptoe Butte. Sick
in that backseat, pop with crackers
churning stomach, thick marijuana
smoke burning my eyes, I aroused
to roll onto the flat, slide out, stand
into the night wind. How like a river
it blew up top—clean, cool, tearing
at my hair, slapping my pants legs.

I watched the others chase across
our butte, one whirling a flashlight
in wild arcs as he bounded circles
round them, his screams all sirens
above the wind: "The sun looping
its silly ass around the sky!" I did
smile pleasure in his hallucination,
in theirs, but my thoughts returned
to you, new friends, who watched,
cuddling quietly together in the car.

From massed rock above the mists
that obscure vision, I stood gazing
up—limited but by distance—saw
clearly and sharply there are more
stars celestial than any mind might

ever hold. That impulse to gesture,
opening arms in praise or embrace
of spellblinding cosmos, or slump
upon my knees, humbling self into
rare dirt—O both seemed so small.

So I just stood in the ripping wind
throbbing a galaxy of stars, abash,
small, shallow, swallowing power.
Another near—spinning, spinning,
head thrown so far back, wheeled
whirls of cosmic lights, staggering
dizzily on limp legs. In whisper he
clutched my arm, hung a-gasp, "O
my God, O my God"—sank to roll
his delusion slow cross the height.

Yes I had to step to that drop edge
and lean into wind, peering across
flatland lamps to the black horizon
and amaze my world does not end
there, and look up again to infinite
lights and astonish it does not end
there. Entranced, I gazed in ritual,
horizon to zenith, zenith to horizon.
Back in the car I did not try to tell
it, but bent quietly from a window
to look up and out now and again.

Two

I find the meaning in this, Mike:
that she has two breasts. Startle in
awe her world does not end there,
and not in a quivered dark cosmos
of her loins—nor away into skies.
There is depth you are plumbing.

And in this, Carol: yes wild wind,
stored in the strengths slung from
his hips, is the same wind that rips
across Steptoe Butte. Dazzle that
it does not end there, nor into sky.
A power is plunging through you.

Not to say or see just a crazed sun,
or myriads, looping and whirling,
though they maybe one day shape
their meaning, but again and again
to die knowing, not understanding
there is forever depth for a plunge.

Three

Oh, you good people, do not cuss
a Puritan upbringing if your ways
cannot be mine, and do not scorn.

There is something more than any
morality: largeness to be visioned
as night view from Steptoe Butte,

that I know but cannot fathom. O
search for something in this poem
while I thrust myself into an open.

FIRST DAY OF AN EIGHT-DAY POEM

Thursday, July 17, 1969, 4:00 PM, Hat Rock near Wallula:
Auto speeding along Lewis & Clark Trail to Spokane,
Columbia blasting through heavens to moon

May we not see God!—Thoreau
A Week on the Concord and Merrimack Rivers

Wake up! I see God
loping across my highway into sagebrush. Coyote—alive
in this Oregon desert—same place, Allen, you
spied him away in the bygone. Scraggy and wily, ol'
Slipp'ry stops to laugh back over-shoulder,
head high, tongue lolling out,
eyes wrinkling.

Yesterday Seattle old book shop—surprise!—
face to face with Suzanna Eve, my palm on her great belly
ready to burst. Last year, lithe,
she kissed her husband, ran off through
Spain and sun with Mr. sly-eyed grinner: bliss-filled
woman, she shimmers.

Frail dark Pamela in Tacoma—mother
of my whelps—trembling, her buzz-cut husband screaming
after me into our starry night:

"What!—drive Eric and Cres to Spokane? Christ!
All these kids know of you is you're some kind of kook
who ties his hair back like a goddamn dog!"

Cheery friends behind in Portland
pickling cucumbers and onions—natural foods recipe. Fresh
dill bouquets our kitchen—garden smell—
and this car. New-peeled orange juicing my hand.
Sage odor heavy in hot air rising
through blue sky.

Do Eagle-men dream
they'll see God alive in the heavens!
Speeding home
to my ten-year (1959 Eagles) high school reunion.
Spokane, where I learned to
dance hard and sneak giddy after the gals. Touch a tit,
then up all night jacking off at the moon.

Look *here!* Coyote—
alive in the flesh
laughing. Like seeing God
with all fours on the earth, tail flagging the wind,
or greeting you in the garden, Allen—
pleasant surprise—
or my own wily image grinning back in puddle shine.

Well, old dog, not so long
since you wild-sang joy in Portland. O after
you slipped away
last blooming—a jammed, jumping May festival night—
flouncy gal tailed me into unlit hallway.

"Hi! My name's Mary Ellen—"
Gets my hair—backs me against staircase—bites.
"Ooww!"
Drags me—"C'mon, asshole!"—by the buckle
upstairs into bathroom.
"I watched you read poems with that bonged-out Ginsberg."
"Oowwww, bitch." Yank the chiffon up—bang
her against unlocked door bouncing
as her husband pushes it.
"Mary Ellen, are you in there!"
Jiz down her thigh. He pops in—snags an arm.
"Let's get out of here. The street's boggled with cops!"
Screams downstairs. We three squirm
a window—crawl over porch—down apple
tree into next yard. Stand
face to face a moment silent in the night. Then dash

away in moonshine,
tiny blossoms flying from our hair.

Radiant Susanna Eve—belly full as the earth, going to bust
any day. Coyote
loping away over the hill laughing:

Ain't no woman gonna git me.
No, no, jus' my good gal.
And she won't git me for long.

Helloooooo! to Roger Thompson—always punched my face
in high school
because we sniffed after the same gals.
After ten years do any fancy to pull my pants down?
Maybe those few apple-eyed tarts sweet to any
boy will be awake and supple,
the others gone fat and timid, scared of joy,
still believe in the Devil, enemies, and other ghosts.

American: We've got an Eagle in space.
We're gonna land a man on the moon, by God, on Sunday
and plant a flag.
Russian: That's nothing. We're landing a man on Mars.
Polack: Hah! we're landing a man on the sun.
American and Russian (laughing): You jackass!
The sun is a gazillion degrees.
Polack: That's where you smart guys get screwed.
We're landing him at night.
Coyote: Oooowwwwwwwwwwwww!

On lone hill late tonight in Spokane after lonesome walk
under Milky Way (clear sky, nighthawks diving):
Great Bear, Little Bear, Eagle, Hare—all the dazzling way to
Great Dog, Little Dog. Eric and Creseyde,
my whelps who know this garden is Paradise.
No beast or angel will ever walk bare-soled and tender
on the moon ground, own heavenly body glistening in earthshine.

Allen, who's layin' low grinning in
bliss-filled woman's twinkled big belly, fleshy
as earth apples? Ask laughing Coyote. Wily ol' dog
slipped away through our scrawny brush.
Listen—over the hill,
old man god wailing the moon.

REV. GARY DAVIS

Black man! blind
as the blues, *whup* and hoot

that shivered head back. Shit! *fwoof*
the false teeth

into your wet damn lap. Just huff,
just *waaa!* Blow bejesus

into guitar jump—thump!—gum that harp
so we clap our thighs.

Yah! I was your boogie-God boy.
Giddy-on-up one you glad chile thangs

on this ol' knee by my big six-string.
Show y'all jus' how a courtin' deacon done.

God old black man! whupping
that guitar one-hand, t'other sliding

your bleach-Bambi's waist. Bounce that
fluffy! Woof that harp out *pwah!*

whup whup way back and
waa! waa! waa! waa! Blondie

slapping your teeth all over
her pink dress.

THE TREES ARE ON FIRE!

Let my son die! He was alive.
I have become you: I cannot teach my boy
the bear and the eagle. You yank ivy
off gravestones, slash grass
from ghost rests.

It's no day for a man to bow. Heart
knifed twice in this bright bite of violet.
My son is dirt. I cannot dance
the eagle. When grandfather stepped for my
father, he hurtled blood
flames shrieking
shrills you can't cry.

Tendons draw legs up
earth pulls them down. Arms
pump a shirt free of slacks. My tie
flows back past an ear. Lungs suck-in this
glacial fall. Furious fuchsia seared red
flares out the chill. Twigs crack under my sole
sharp as shots.

I am Mule Deer! Spruce smacks
my breast as I leap. I'm alive till I die
sailing this siren splash slap so yellow-orange.

The trees are on fire! Grandfather pranced
his eagle three suns before those legs
would sleep. There is nothing
but this fierce air sucked
into the lungs and
that crisp burst
ablaze in
the dying
limbs.

JUST ABOVE ANY LITTLE TOWN

Now breathe deep

and lift the story
as you do your arms, saying
ahh yes this
is good day down over the brush-
covered slopes soaked
with mist
since earliest

memory. Here come

two housewives
out under one umbrella
to walk their primal fat off sparkling
in fire and cream
sweaters—while dogs just
descended from wolves
flash past

them. So wily

as time a young bare-
chested professor whinnies his
naked baby
along below these wild yucca wands
sprung out into flower,
where so fiercely we shake
droplets off our

glasses. In vivid

mist you are
already up the slope
back against a log beside some
whiskery uncle,
hooting as sparks snap out
through jumps in smoke and vapor
to be stars of the sky

all over again.

BIRTH OF THE SKIN

On the street
a blind girl glides

before me like the shadow

from a cloud.
And all of my skin

lives. Out through raw vapor

in a crest of fireflies. O yes here
beyond those green and holy

gills at the godhead.

Girl! Blind girl!
Come forth

up out from me, opening now

these hands stretched
on ahead of my

sea-lit face.

WHAT IS SLEEP

transcribed from taped live improvisation

sleep is the brain of a flower
sleep is your last chance to open like a parachute
sleep is a train with gold windows coming over a waterfall
sleep is that long sled ride down a snowy hill
sleep is the star at the bottom of my beer
sleep is an elephant kneeling to a child with a sparkler
sleep is the castle you were born in
sleep is in love with the butterfly of my lips
sleep is a horse nobody else can ride
sleep is the desert at night on a lunchbox pressed to our heart
sleep is the journal of God
yes
that's what sleep is

sleep is a nun driving a tractor into a snowstorm
sleep is a stop sign in flames
sleep is a semi rolling wide open through a cathedral
sleep is the highway away from my head
sleep is glowing like any tailpipe in the stars
sleep is a loose ribbon falling from the sky
sleep is a balcony full of soldiers tossing rose petals and panties
sleep is the lost dress that floats
sleep is a blind sailor who kisses like a woman
sleep is that milk you thought you'd never get again
sleep is not ours to keep
sleep is where the wind went

sleep
what is sleep

fog in a cat's mouth

      popcorn on a lamb's back

            a cloud in an elevator

sleep is a Cadillac with a hood full of doves
sleep is a watermelon kissed by a priest

sleep is a hot
flashlight to my heart
as I swim to the cellar with
my red eyes glowing

HELLO!

This is a Bengali! Something terrible
has happened! This is Ramakrishna. Do you have a
pencil? You may be needed in San Francisco. The chosen
lotus has been electrocuted at
Dammasch Hospital by Dr. William Thompson
of Portland. Take down this number—*12490*—the lost case cipher.
And this abductee slide out of the solar system: *KZQc²*.
We are going to need photographs
of Swami Aseshananda, a pretender to flare
wildly important for seven weeks. At least 5000 photographs.
Anne Gerety is the next incarnation but
she is no longer of our species. Running chrome-color
shots are absolute proof
of crawler presence on the planet.
We have tape recording of Dr. Thompson's family
by mental telepathy. Over 4000 years of teachings—are lost!
Our whole world is under abductee hypno-
cranium-graphing from the Crab nebula. You may have to pack up
and leave. Duck all splashes
of publicity. Dr. Thompson might like to know he has
killed Christ. I am really praying you can validate
some radio-astronomers. Do you speak Bengali? You must
shoot the crawler over and over with
a flash-enhanced pink Kodak Instamatic 104.
Bengies are the only ones left who can help—the closest global
language to Uranian. Our next level of evolution is *their*
radio cone. If you are approached
by Bengalis who do not blink,
tell them *Christ is on the Funnel 90.* Tell them *Stop the shock table.*
Tell them *Let us see some of the documents.* Wait a minute.
One moment. The baby
has just been born. But he may morph. These little
baby disciples have got to stop. It's all up to you. Shoot those
chromes and wink away in time
to warn shock-blocked lotus breeding pools.

Crawlers will be screwing earthlings into vices to suck
out what remains of our sodium. You will soon
be meeting your jump teacher. Do you
know what I mean? Are you
writing this down?

CORNISH INSTITUTE
OF ALLIED ARTS

George is laughing
at Catherine on her back
for today's life-drawing ingénues,
naked but the lone silvered spike-heel
dangling from a toe, that ankle
balanced up across her bent
knee. So our maestro
aims his phono needle down
as he laughs perfectly into Gene Autry
crooning *Irene, goodnight.*
And you are floated
out by such a sudden gust
like some snowfallen angel among
a glare of bicycles,
so blinded with laughter
you cannot bliss how dearly
two swallows love
swoops and rolls they go on looping
away over your dancing pencil.

THE CLOSING

With eyes we
tease and ravish. We hold . . .
lusting in our lust

until I reach to push away
fallen curls as you pull
my face to engorged
nipples my eyes
kiss, witching
shiver to your groin.

Spark eyes
in our palms blink quivered
to the breasts, our loins,
fluttered ai! stuttered

until all eyes close
in that spasm
last flash

yours rolled back
where mine can't hold them . . .

I'm floating. Am I there?
Can you kite me
pulling to the ceiling

Only then do you drift
beyond our lips.

STUMBLING INTO THE DARK

After William Stafford's "Traveling into the Dark"

Crashing down in rapids, slammed onto a ledge,
I clawed up piled rock to grapple at a hand
half God's—and pulled choking to his face
who sprawled in wild bloom and twilight thaw.

I heaved just to my knees. Here fell our poet,
that master through clouds and clumps of snow
stepping down this run to chant on solstice eve
—when his heart plunged in somersault like me.

Blossoms scattered as I lurched up in gasping
stagger. Way on down beside this mountain's
holy flow, they'll hand round broth and blood,
each leap the flames, and call for every poem.

That mouth fell open while I swayed. A star
streamed coldly off. Can I last, old man,
I prayed—staring dead on down the darkening
path—and tumble to their arms like you?

I waited as for words, all lost in shiver—
then shoved him over blossoms into the river.

5. Jesus Wept

OPHELIA

Sea of Norway, midnight, spring 1037 A.D.

I step alone through this windless night
plank after plank, lean blistered railing
to flat, black water. If these sails pulse,
it is sorcery. A wreathed moon shivers
ribbons into swell. All current empties
somehow to such a sea. Somehow she
has ghosted me here. O it is her shine
wrinkling the depths. *Ophelia, pluming
child, you misunderstood!* Now but water
chimes flat and black beneath our stars.

Haunting fragrance of her rising gown
bells up bubbled fathoms, a resonating
aria from an unfastened world. It pulls
my heart right out as pure mists of rain.
A blowing whale halos, rolling up dark
churn, moon billowed into pale whorls.
Our stars breathe—and wavelets wake
splashes of hushed laughter. That deep
soul has glanced her, tumbling the long
unfurling veils in roiled ballet. *Ophelia!*

But with my cry, he sounds her plunge,
all timpani. When swirls go there is no
breath, no riffle, only fainted refraction
fluttered under a lift of wash. How easy
to spill like her—into a spiral of specter
song and funnel to where she pirouettes.
*Ophelia—but a bloom!—you could not
understand.* Now O! you have left only
shimmers of wreath ringing out from a
black water, our stars awake in distance.

THE NAMES

These are the names
of my horses
and sons. These are their names.

Mick. Max. Cracker. Mallory.
Hay-boy. Horace. Swish. Chip. Pippin.
Nicko. Dicker. Delmar.
Darlen. Spookla. Ambrose. Ross.

These are the names
of my daughters
and shrubs. These are the names
of my opening flowers.

Rosette. Betsy. Maribeth. Rosemary. Mae.
Moll. Holly. Heather. Belle.
Britt. Margaret. Pip. Pansy. Sarah.
Mary Sharon. Maud.
Arlene. Dawn. Rhoda.

These are the names
of my aunts
and great-aunts and these are the names
of my kissing cousins.

Olga. Iris. Eileen. Nan. Violet.
Lanette. Alice. Babs. Betty Jo. Lois. Flo.
Trish. Dixie. Roxanna.
Dot. Darlene. Floss. Fanny.
Pretty Pat. Squirt. Sis.

These are the names
of my bosoms and buddies.
These are the names and the names
of my road pardners.

Darlin' Bill. Lily. Dick-a-lick. Luther
Spook. Spiff. Sparkla. Martha Wong.
Johnny-the-Blondie. Indian Ronnie. Real
Grace. Jim. Jerusalem Slim.
Slam. Ghostman. Horseheart Nick. Chip. Okie
Mickey. Sissy. Rosio Cozy.

And these are the names
of my brothers
and lovers. These are the names.

Mick. Spic. Spook. Slit.
Slant. Wetback. Dyke. Cracker. Squaw. Scum.
Midget. Maggot. Grit.
Grunt. Slut. Lush. Trash. Spaz-ass.
Chippie. Nigger-hips. Swish.
Shitkicker. Dicklicker.
Darling. Darling. Darling.

HER CAROL ON THE BULLET

Across aisle
our eyes spark like
this *Streak* at Christmas
flash!—*whooo!*—flash!—funneling
whiteout Alps. Whosits slips
from a woozy fiancé
into these thundered darks
of—uhhh!—such up high blizzard lightning
flash!—*uh!*—*whoo!*—*uh!*—flash!
as under our coats
we slam like dogs not caring who sees—
so many shadowy arms flinging
flash!—flying!—flash!
up—*whoooo!*—from our shrieking
peacoats.

FLIGHT OF MY SOUL

Twilight, Night, Up into Dawn

Owww! Bobby Byrd
old Ford half up an oak, bonged
your head off that dash, slammed from behind
by *la Mami Superior,* her trunk popped,
wetbacks springing out, cops foiled in circles,
while you dial Lee, yell her car is creamed, which tree,
so you'll be home a tad after, *kiss kiss,* gotta run
two miles of white-line, late for that poetry,
slapping away asphalt. Run!

Jolts of heart up an aisle
parting startled spectators, you pacing so
boinged, the adrenaline whirling
your words, starbursts torn out rose-violet sky, surged
shoot-from-your-belly blurt—hyeah!—as up-gusts
sucked from those toes, soles,
churning this earth. That dean piñatas
"The g-guy's nuts! He's b-b-blown it all to snot."
Bobbing on out, you hurl back jaws on high
"Wad your donkey job up the bum!
I'm gonna run! run! my
El Paso
home to tell Lee
Wail your clarinet!"

"I'm gonna run
to Juárez!" Lee in that slip
out on the porch stuffing waitress tips
into your pockets. "I gotta *go!"*
Your kids in the yard fallen around your knees
on roller-skates, hugging jumpy legs, pratting back on
skinny butts. Lee laughs to her next-door
"Yo! our old Bobby-o! He's off running to Juárez!"
Laughs back, *"Aie! Yi!* Lee, paying for *that?"*
Those kids all roller-skating
downhill toward the *Río* after you . . .

fade into *sueño*
while Lee streams in her slip
"Run, Bobby Byrd! Run!"

So many neighbors
out on porches under Milky Way
cascading north down to south *como rapidos . . .*
Nada so good on TV as cheering those border guards
chasing wetbacks out of our *Río Grande*
into *Tejas,* as you glance
a lit-up city bus
slow for jump-on *mestizo-cholo-chuco*
chingados. Galloping by, three white horses moonlit
without saddles, bouncing a woman, her *niñita*
under arm, *norte,* the *marido*
y bravados sprinting—*pinché si!*—as we
shriek up glee.

You, Bobby, burst
into *la Ciudad,* a ripped blitz of
Spanglish past your dumbstruck customs chums.
Always that handslap or snap out the
Dos Equis . . .
for one more aimless slide
into snakeknots of street. *Yi!* leaping high
yelps, *el santo loco de* stunned
Indios y Mexicanos squatting cobbles to proffer
"*Chiclettes, cigarettes,*" little wraps of pumpkin seeds.
Slapped up guitars, accordion cry, a
far sweet clarinet sway.
La puta guera stomping strappy spikes
in purple *culottes* with a twirling *cocinero*
de grillos, his grin twisted
aslant by knife swipe.

Our ruined buses, *mas* rusty
taxicabs left chugging like fast babble
to follow you. Run, Bobby. Romp *la promenad*
round and round their *monumento inmenso de mármol*

al Benito, splatting
Dos Equis across our bowed skulls,
slinging pumpkin seeds as grackles flock
up—flapping and squawking—glistened in blue-green
purplish sheen. *Go!* those chop-voiced screechers
bursting so terrified as you wing
through all a-flap
screaming "*Gracias! Gracias! Gracias!*"

WELCOME TO THE ALPHABET

El Paso toward Bisbee, November 20, 1980

Just after Rodeo, New Mexico,
wheeling upon the Arizona line, I startle
having motored through desert, cactus everywhere,
my first time. Suddenly!
an open field of bright orange
pumpkins—scattered randomly throughout
glisten black cows. I gasp, coasting by, my head
turned back. Then
the sign
Welcome to Arizona!
backlit by wretched skyline.
Yi! aie si! A huge black bull, dick dragging
the ground, kissing this earth.
I could roar off
my asphalt
into that ongoing *si!* unfathomable,
were there an ocean— or just head-on that blackest
glaring god-horned beast all ink . . . and wake
beside, Dick kissing the dirt
swelling under bright orange pumpkins,
black cows scattered all among . . .
in this sunlight . . .
of a desert.

RATBASTARD

"Yo! Barhop!"
Bangs his shotglass.
Another Cuervo!"
Sour Stetson crushed down
over his squints purpled with bruises.
"Two slops José Gold
trumps a redhead with a rump
spitting *Shut up!*"
He slams his jigger, twists of hair
stuck to blood in the crease
at his mouth.
"I damn can't stomach a man stumbles gaga
into a cloud of perfume."
Slams his knuckles.
Jibes out the droop mustache
glint busted teeth.
Hoists the next Gold burst,
chile splatters, spray from two noses
blossoming his stink of a shirt
like stomped roses.
"This hot swallow of blue agave
beats any flame-hair bitch
in a nose job shrieking
Ratbastard!"
Slams it.
"I don't give a sneeze of posies. By god
she can choke on her own
unholy blaze!"
His gashed fist waves
the glass.
"Ohh you won't catch me, not me
with a faceful. "He bangs
it. "Gimmee the slug
of mescal with a worm that'll gag that
Kodiak she's
blinding her ass out for now."
Slams it. Slams it.

THE LYRIC MIST OF FACES

Cristi Luna mask-making workshops summer 2001

Of raindrops, of freckles,
of wet streaks below your eyes flowing
all that ink and lipstick, of papyrus smeared like some rippling
camisole kissed awake birthday after birthday
to layer our rapt masques in a wrinkling of laughter
and mortal gasp.

With your countenance
illuminated like dread's own comet
crashing into my breast, of the canons of doves outside
an open window in the rain of pages that we believed had been lost
beyond all those flaming wings seared between
our lips . . .

To let go and float
is forever the twisting of stars in our cries.
In bliss and tears just above that Hell
streaming away all paste and faith wreathed in those nettings
we lift up like a daughter's lacey underneath, eyelashes and smoke dear
to the pounded heart. To give up
your throat and its blossom blurring into that mirror
always sobbing back. To release full those blooms with one shriek
that vanishes birthmark, freckle, ripple, wrinkle, dimple as a
layer of sky peeled away.

JESUS WEPT

After that 1925 Aeolian Hall premier of Aaron Copland's
Symphony for Organ and Orchestra, *Nadia Boulanger*
as organ soloist, conductor Walter Damrosch turned to his
audience and confided that when Nadia had asked Virgil
Thompson, important critic and composer, why he'd wept.
upon first hearing it, Virgil answered, "Because I had not
written it myself!" Then Damrosch stepped to his edge and
said so infamously, "Ladies and gentlemen, I am sure you
will agree that if a gifted young man can write a symphony
like this at twenty-three, within five years he will be ready
to commit murder." So all of that evoked what now follows.

He spied sunlight dancing
Mozart's young brow. Below a lark rising
from the daisied field he kissed that white fur around
a mouse's eyes. And Jesus wept.

He gulped a hooting plumber
toss his awakened daughter skyward
into snowflakes floating brightened against burst stars.
He inhaled a seamstress in full shrieking flicker
of her jet Singer needle
dinging crazily an unknown *Ave Maria.*
And Jesus wept.

He tasted fragrance
of lilies in those tattooed arms of his holy suicide two
iridescent ravens leered upon from her lip of
reddened ditch. O he sprang our earth
for orphans heartbroken by beauty. So truly Jesus
wept, hands out
for a sparkled hanging artist
head-swept from spotlit trapeze.

Outside over the bluff
a sunset of roses
cast shadows longing toward
that waif who had become such a catapulted violinist

sailing chocolates in his scarlet heart
across those rapids to a loved threshold. A ribbon
of quail dashed gravel into wavering grass
while my blue ride sliced it away.
And Jesus wept.

Oil rippled the river as a Toyota tilted
deeper, baby inside squealing at kisses popping toes.
Ohh! Mummy mouthed bubbles, swirled in
riverweed, slapping at glass,
eyes so big. Like Azrael's glint, a bluebottle fly
squatted the body of a dapple fawn.
Jesus wept and wept.

All purrs in slumber-lap
of our cozy great aunt rocking before flames,
that calico fuzzy crackling in static
with onrush of those low thunder strikes—explodes!
as sparks blasted down the
chimney and outland stallions stampeded
ahead of high-leaping grassfire.
And Jesus wept.

The cold creek went on
streaming, cutthroat gasping for snowmelt,
gills slashed orange in wet grass of
a dripping creel. As Peter lied through her teeth
that she lifted old solace like lace from the Holy Grail,
he thrust aloft his one starburst slipped
onto finger after finger.
And Jesus wept.

Blossomed in blood
I just rolled wild shrieking *Sweet*
Pea! stabbed in my throat,
in my eye, both ankles and heart while
jitter-hop dancing, some flutterbug shimmied
pheromones along a radiant blade. Oh didn't you spot
monarchs skimming that heavenly

pink of our viscera ringing girdlethorn like
Christmas daybreak
when Jesus had yet to weep!

Herbert—professor of luminous
lingo, in silk pajamas transfixed by *Clair de Lune,*
who adored Falstaff, Grendel, Puck,
a rollicking Wife of Bath—
trussed wrist to ankle racked so far back by
burglary as translucent Great Blues resounding waves
from PJs all flashed upshrieked wings. O Jesus
wept as Herbert gagged for his precious
he had named long
before tonight's slight door tapping—maybe
her! Penelope Snowblossom.

Thus this ecstatic delicacy
of an ever-expanding colossal cosmos,
astoundingly perfected in its own ethereal serendipity
down to that tiny machinery
of an orange-wing Tarantula Hawk tapping
to pique the T-Rex of arachnids up out of its burrow
grappling to rapt paralysis, stabbed
by an amber wasp.
She lays one egg in that softly pulsing
underbelly. And stunned warmth calls forth into
heartbeat a hatchling that devours
day by day
a snug still a-dream cadaver . . .
until joyously blinding out so damn orange
into this splendorous dazzle of our own shimmery
reality. Where Jesus wept. He wept.
Yes wept. O he wept.

WATER DOG

Head Bartender, El Cobre Lounge, San Jose Lodge,
Bisbee, AZ, three miles from Mexico, May 18, 1986

Yo! Water Dog! a shot of Cuervo
Silver! Toss me some Pall Malls. Splash drinks
for every hombre here. Charlie, Doc,
what's your poison?

Streaming in from rosy blasts
of sundown, I see their glory nail
glint. Oh I know that rubber salamander
hammered to the high cordials shelf—all splayed
lipsdown—is spit on me.

Ain't it so, Water Dog!
That smelter was here before those sissy
do-goodies was even born. If it's so
goddam pretty where they fart from, why don't
they just pack up their hair and
hump on back?

So many dreams before
this, I really do wake after all night to envision
a gasping lizard spiked to a post
hung staring to me, that plump tongue
red as a heart clamped scarlet in its mouth
dripping brightness.

Water Dog! Flip on the tube!
We gonna see us some smash-face. Weeooooo!
Ho! Ricky-Tic, ten smackers says blackest
one gets a bomb to that hog snout.
What? Ya don't like sport, Water Dog?

Dr. Silver, he's just gotta shine
a new pumpshot, a pickup, a ranch house and pool,
another racehorse. So he swings me inverted
strapped to a stainless slab, gleaming

110

needle punched in my spine,
eyeing the screen flicker barium so radiantly
toward my only brain.

Hey, Doc! a Nigger, a Mex, a Gook
get throwed off the Grand Canyon at a same heartbeat.
Which one splats bottom first?   *Huh?*
Well, who cares! Ha! ha! ha! Right, Water Dog!

I'm little steps in back of a sheriff,
my scared eyes just behind his gun butt and bullets
over that ditch beside a cornfield to witness
in resplendence honey-red
hair on my Flame punctured and wriggled by maggots,
her long ears, flag tail stiff against dirt.

Goddammit, Water Dog! I wish
we'd just go clusterfuck
those sandshitters to nuke hell! Let the jolly Allah
sort them out. Jesus bleeding Christ, kill
the news, Water Dog. Crank
up that juke. So we can sock us some
country stomp-it.

Do the years cry by
as we stand entwined—sobbing, slipping
through time. My grandma is all pulse in black rayon
sparked with light, my eyes hugged
wet against the slobbered dress. We're choking
to empty our hearts of Flame.

Water Dog! Dump another
splot of hot Silver! And whatever
that little Missy down at your end wants. Hell, just
splash one for everybody. What's your
poison, Honey?

Strychnine—it rips
through gut like napalm. Oh she writhes and mews—

finally stiffens her four legs beside
this white-daisy ditch as a thousand flies hymn
into hair my hands loved.

I don't shiv a git, Water Dog!
I said dump her a drink. It don't mean a Gook what
she don't want. She'll spread 'em—
Her mama did. Let it squat in front of her
till she bloats.

I never do bury my Flame
but run and run. That sheriff surely
is dragging her away. I sprint straight across
blossomed fields to where Grandma waits weeping at
end of our gravel, both arms out.

Water Dog, don'cha just
love to hear them sobbing those nasty
little hearts out when you hunker to pound on
home? Jesus I'd like to nail one down so she wouldn't
never get up. Hey! I'm no bigot.
I'll fuck a Nigger. I'll fuck a Spic. I'll fuck a Chink.
But I'd never vote for one. Would
we, Water Dog?

Silver punches the hole sloppy,
yanks out, spikes me again
I leak spinal fluid all these weeks while
he knows but is too enraptured stacking his dollars
as my brain splits and I swim across a floor in
vomit and nightmares.

Just ask Water Dog—if that gash
gets Vice Prez, she'll be stinking the rag
or laughing over puppies
when she oughta be bazooking the Ruskies and faggots.
Christ, you'll prob'ly vote for her, Water Dog.

As I stand gazing into sparkling zenith
from this cornrow now again in flower, straddling the
ditch that must be her grave
I wonder how I could've ever been a child
with my own Flame.

Water Dog! Hit me double
with Silver. Oh hell yes!—pitch me
one last pack of those coffin nails. Hallelujah! Missy,
I'm hammered tonight. One for every goddamn
caballero here.

Yes Sir! and
I let the Silver slosh and
begin to heat this shot in my fist
as I slide it before him like holy water while Doc's
lighter flares over his grin lit up forever.
I look back for that flickering screen
where brightness burns down
gullet to gut a-shine
right through these pearl-button shirts
rising to each heart a glow.
Toward any brain blazes a nimbus
around one liver, and one more, shimmying
elbow to elbow along the bar, every big-belted waist
in halo, a name to grace it—*Doc, Bud,*
Ricky-Tic, Charlie, Billy, Buell, Jack—to blop
through each catcaller's stool
onto spattered floor in bubble and smoke.
At last it hisses through
flashing
our bombed hearts, all souls, our love
sucked so deep we may never find home. Suddenly
shoots a nova blinding whorls
out past dogs and half-breeds and Gooks and grandmas
to incandescent childhood
sliding down dead, dead as nails,

dead as a dog, as backbones alive in napalm,
down down down,
a dazzling whole whooping flamed dive
delirious on into Hell.

What? Cat got'cha by the tongue, Water Dog?

WHEEL DEMON

These wheelchair people around NW Portland
give me bat shivers, middle of night, stuck in a
railroad crossing, who knows why or how long,
one guy sitting at the top of an on-ramp in that
industrial district waiting for a semi to pull out.
     —Katherine Dunn to DB 9/17/79

Out of night
wind flares the butt in his teeth,
ashes sparking back, as he rolls down at you
with such hate in that glare, coke-bottle specs lit up
like high beams, a grin of silver braces
as glinted as diesel grill. Christ! what's that—
black book under his pit
flying a new satin
marker? Fifth of Jack snugged
up his crotch, chair chromed out, shining
like an Edsel.
Tattoos snake round arms
muscled as a mobster's, gashed in his
backrest
Adios, muthafuck!
Upthrust finger as he whishes
by me a-gasp in a ditch,
chops one more notch in that right
wood thigh. Flaming his black tee, pack tucked
up a sleeve, fluorescent death's head in goggles, glaze
helmet, bolt splitting Dickie's own ticker
winging at forehead,
blood bandana.
That rickety chair in high
whine spinning free as sin, near past hearing.
Throat thrown open to howl, his
own hound loping after, haggard and lean
as Hell. Ohhhh! you sweeeet *hearts,* you're gonna
snap right up in your Caddy Cushion
when that weeping
reaper comes shrieking
down upon you.

MAGGIE

Her shit Ford
heater on the fritz
loaded out for Capistrano
three kids, two cats, all
she could cram in or squirrel-knot
on top—in that freaking East Coast sleet.
Witch's tit on through Tulsa
where her claustrophobic calico choked up a hairball
onto the tabby. Ju-ju's shrieked shake-off shot
vomit into snap-freeze clots against glass,
gumming Maggie's hair and all those
snugged navy surplus watch caps.
The windshield, side views
streaked until
San Diego sunglasses,
cats both sleep-twitching, paws
into the breezy, three donut-powdered
lovebuds crashing through
sandcastles,
swallows circling in.

LEARNING TO DRIVE

—Go, go, go, everybody!
Bill Haley & the Comets, 1955

—Here Dad laughs
and I shoot my arm straight out into
Sunday. Sax-honks rock
the radio.
I wheel this Chevy in sunlight, roll
off onto a long, disappearing country road.
In the rearview a cloud
of our best summer is pouring up
behind.
—Easy he says. *Easy.*
It goes forever.
He's here to
show me everything there is
as we sweep between these fields
like the silver tracks.
—Now try your horn.

Suddenly—
bolting from Dad's
side, a sunstruck buck, eyes
wild, plunges
alongside our blue door, pulling hard
ahead.
—Step it down
Dad gasps.
Boy
hands to the wheel,
I'm thrust
forward, up to that driving
rump.
—Faster. Go.
With the neck, Lord the neck, horns
in sunburst. My leg

and the engine
explode through all radio.
I look
across Dad half-out his window
into that bulging eye.
—*Go!*
Sax-honks, Dad slapping
the door, nostrils flared, huge chest
heaving, all
lungs
and combustion. —*Go!*
Go! Go!

This is the way
in thunder
down a bright road of dust
we dip
eye to gold eye—and up
over cinders and track   sail   heart to
our throats

on one   glorious   rising   wail

like the whole blue
sky has opened. Our buck away into hayfield

leaps sunflashed, farther and farther
as I let up the gas
before Dad stops whooping
out the window.

And anyone

laughing down from the sky
surely sees Dad's hand
on the dash—great plumes still trailing

as we sweep into
this field and that, out of a world
that needs nothing from us
more . . .

all the horns blaring
—*I love you.*

Go. I love you all.

BUDDY HOLLY BIRTHDAY PARTY

Long Goodbye Tavern, Portland, Oregon, Sunday 9/16/79

Don't tell me
God doesn't wear
sunglasses. Gowned out into the dirt
as a blaze of radiance,
eyes lifted, Oh!
you gawk Him hopping with that
pink shirt open, finger-pops two like-a me—
day suédes flashing
whack-step to my rush
of pulse,
backup host
rumping those robes
across a glare of sky-shined floor
yipping the electric lick.
Whoa! didn't I know there was just nothing
but rock and bop, my kicks flying
up—*Yip!*—like His.
Ain't a lot, is it!— is it!—
but everything to me. Jesus! I was off
with a chop of my
digits. Now here I spring out O
is there really—*Yip!*—some coming thunder!
lightning! footwork so fright'ning!
Christ! that'll be the oh boy!
So I was right as rapture, up off my ass,
that stripped glistening
hotcharged into the incarnate heart
—Eddie, me, Ritchie—
our damn dance leaping this
whole world of shock
to a stomping Boss.

Best guess for birth date September 7, 1936.
Charles Hardin Holley childhood nickname
"Buddy." Decca Records 1956 contract in
error "Holly," Buddy decided looked better.
Ritchie Valens, May 13, 1941–Feb. 3, 1959.
Eddie Cochran, Oct. 2, 1938–Apr. 17, 1960.

INDEX

POEM PAGE NUMBER & DATE OF CONCEPTION, FIRST NOTES, INITIAL DRAFT

CHRONOLOGICAL DATE OF CONCEPTION, FIRST NOTES, INITIAL DRAFT

ALSO BY DICK BAKKEN

BOOKS

Hungry!, contemporary avant-garde Bengali poets, with commentary by guest editor Howard McCord, Jyotirmoy Datta, Carol Berge, Allen Ginsberg, Gary Snyder, others, influential mimeographed perfect bound book on six colors of paper, Salted Feathers, Portland, Oregon, 1967, 124 pp., 500 copies, **o.p.**

Miracle Finger. A Book of Works by Children Ages Two to Fifteen with Notes by Parent and Teacher Poets (Bakken, Philip Dow, Gwen Head, Sandra McPherson, Primus St. John, several others), by offset press with photos and artwork, Salted Feathers, Portland, Oregon, 1975, 80 pp., 1000 copies, **o.p.**

Here I Am, book-length poem, 18 photos by 6 photographers of poem's performance by Bakken with dancer Susan Vernier, by offset press, St. Andrews Press, Laurinburg, North Carolina, 1979, 40 pp. 1000 copies, **o.p.**

Feet with the Jesus, poetry collection, offset press, Lynx House Press, Amherst, Massachusetts, 1989, 52 pp., 100 sailcloth over boards with adaesio art by Abigail Rorer, 900 paper copies.

Dick Bakken: Greatest Hits 1967–2002, by offset press, Pudding House Publications, Columbus, Ohio, 2005, 40 pp., 1st ed. 250 copies.

Where Is America Going! / The Columbine Body Count, Island Hills Books, Chino Valley, Arizona, online website, 10,000 words, 2007.

NON-LETTERPRESS CHAPBOOKS, PAMPHLETS, BOOKLETS

True History of the Eruption, photocopy limited edition of 25, Portland, Oregon, 1980, 24 pp., **o.p.**

Spring Day, postcard, in *Merlyn Gorky,* vol. I, no. 2, 24 poemcards, San Francisco, 1980, **o.p.**

Last Will and Testament, single-poem booklet, Suburban Wilderness Press, Duluth, Minnesota, 1988, 6 pp., 300 copies, **o.p.**

Yes I Am! / An American Medley, HP Officejet tri-color pamphlet, Heart of Carlos Spoken Arts, Bisbee, Arizona, 2004, 76 copies.

Song, HP Officejet facsimile edition of DB "Song" from John Dennis original 1975 limited edition photo-poem postcard [next list], Heart of Carlos Spoken Arts, Bisbee, Arizona, 2004, 70 copies.

Catching Her Blue Ribbons, HP Officejet postcard, Heart of Carlos Spoken Arts, 2005, 25 copies.

LETTERPRESS, FOLDOVERS, BROADSIDES, POSTCARDS, EPHEMERA

Song, photo-poem postcard, John Dennis, Portland, Oregon, 1975, 29 signed, numbered copies, **o.p.**

How to Eat Corn, single-poem yellow booklet in blue envelope, covers Canson Mi Tientes, text pages Velin Arches, hand-sewn letterpress limited edition, Carrington Press at September Press, London, England, 1986, 100 numbered copies, **o.p.**

The Coming of Spring, single-poem rolled scroll tied by thin rain-blue ribbon, letterpress limited edition, on handmade Italian paper with handmade Japanese paper envelope, Carrington Press at September Press, England, 1986, 86 numbered copies, **o.p.**

Grace, poem by letterpress on bright orange postcard, now it's up to you publications, Denver, Colorado, 1988, 1000 copies, **o.p.**

Tree, single-poem Wheat-Thins-size tiny booklet in tiny envelope, hand-sewn letterpress limited edition, Carrington Press, Maple Valley, Washington, 1988, 188 numbered copies, **o.p.**

The Coming of Spring, special occasion letterpress broadside, translucent cover sheet, Carrington Press, Maple Valley, Washington, limited edition 10 numbered copies, sold out at event, 3/19/89, DB with dancer Donna Ribka, Divergent Arts Poetry Series, MARS Artspace, Phoenix, Arizona, **o.p.**

Going into Moonlight, single-poem booklet with envelope, hand-sewn letterpress limited edition, on special papers, with gold ink, embossing, artwork, Carrington Press, Maple Valley, Washington, 1990, 300 numbered copies.

Jesu O Jesu, eight-poem booklet, hand-sewn letterpress edition on special papers with cover etching by Isabee Thiebaut tipped into embossed impression, Ringdove, Berkeley, California, 1990, 12 pp., 500 copies.

Poem of the Guest, file-folder-label-size loose-leaf booklet in envelope with special papers and blind-embossed cricket, letterpress limited edition, Carrington Press, Maple Valley, Washington, 1998, 198 numbered copies.

Twin Towers, a two-poem set, loose-leaf tall booklet with special meadow-green translucent papers, Carrington Press, Maple Valley, Washington, Spring 2003, 111 numbered copies.

AUDIO CASSETTES

Kazuko Shiraishi with Dick Bakken, Pima College, Tucson, September 24, 1984, with KS poem "My Tokyo" performed by KS, DB, Dennis Williams, stereo audio cassette, 60 minutes, Brushfire Publications, Phoenix, Arizona, 1985, 150 copies, reissued in new packaging July 2003, 35 copies.

The Other Side: Dick Bakken Live, 22 selections from performances 1978–1984 around the USA, stereo audio cassette, 60 minutes, Brushfire Publications, Phoenix, Arizona, 1986, 350 copies, reissued in new packaging July 2003, 50 copies.

New Letters on the Air / Contemporary Writers on Radio / Dick Bakken, catalog # 19901019, recorded by New Letters at KCUR-FM, Kansas City, Missouri, April 23, 1990, with moderator Rebekah Presson, 29 minutes, 1990.

FILM AND STAGE PRODUCTIONS

Book of the Cur: Dick Bakken, Poet, 20-minute Betamax videotape featuring photos of DB, biography, poetics, live voicing of poems "Note to the Institution," "Hymn," "The Happy Birthday House," Bev Walton director, Portland, Oregon, 1973.

Poet Dick Bakken: Customer Objects to Neck, Carol Papalas director, Zoe Video Productions Presents Arizona Arts, Bakken's 5/9/87 Broadview Motel, Mesa, Arizona, performance of his poem, 10 minutes.

Oregon / a Video by Jack Estes from a Poem by Dick Bakken, 1988 performance of the poem at Peninsula College, Port Angeles, Washington, 4 minutes interspersed with actor Morris Bond and background bar band Gary Heffern and the Cunninghams singing their "Two-Bit Dames," 1990.

Miracle Finger / Here I Am / by Dick Bakken, a multi-media performance based on works by children, starring adults and children, a benefit for children with learning challenges, Gorilla Theatre Productions in Cooperation w/ The Stimulus & Response Co., The Human Observation Lab, Kansas City, Missouri, 1990, 12 shows April 12–28.

DB's "Wedding Gift: Four Spoons, a Jar of Honey, Dried Rosehips," choreographed by Marian Runyeon, spoken by T. Greg Squires, acoustic guitar by Don Reeve, Cabaret Theatre, Temple of Music & Art, Tucson, Arizona, March 28, 29, 30, 1991, "Zenith Dance Collective Presents Views from the Zenith," reviewed in *The Arizona Daily Star*, Fri., March 29, 1991, by Gene Armstrong: "*Wedding Gift*, an intriguing investigation into marriage . . . Bakken's poem illustrated the unexpected strangeness with which we occasionally view our lover. Squires and Runyeon's duet abstracted the ensuing alienation, confusion and sweet fascination—it was perfect for the space."

Goanna, color 20-minute VHS film, stage performance by Bakken with dancer Caryl Clement, musician Will Clipman, Tokyo poet Kazuko Shiraishi, at *Monsoon* Bisbee Poetry Festival 1992. Bakken won a $5,000 Artist Projects Grant from

Arizona Commission on the Arts to create this interdisciplinary, multimedia production based on Shiraishi's poem "Goanna God" (*Goanna* is Australian Aboriginal for "Lizard"). Clipman plays dijeridu (Aboriginal wind instrument), water drums, other primitive instruments. Shiraishi's poem is voiced in dramatic interplay of Japanese–English by Kazuko and Bakken. Costumes by James Loveland, lighting by Russell Stagg, rigging by Ross Philip. Clement, the Lizard in Loveland's magnificent costume creation, does surprise upside down entrance and exit via cable. Three-camera shoot filmed, edited, produced by Evelyn Boatright. Shown 8 times on cable channel 62, 8 times on cable channel 49, Tucson, Arizona, 1992–1993, shown with David Chorlton's introductory interview with Bakken, *Outrage & Excellence*: Dimension Cable channel 22, Phoenix-Tempe-Mesa-Chandler, Arizona, aired 4 times in 1993.

SELECTIONS FROM EXHIBITIONS & ART

DB's "Wayne's Poem," "Uncle Lloyd," "Marcia and Theresa," Isabee Thiebaut [now Demski] monoprint "Pinch Ass" + 3 more, *The Yellow Magazine*, Fall 1975, ed. Mark Seeley, "excerpts from *Pinch Ass* / a work-in-progress / poems by Dick Bakken / monoprints by Isabee Thiebaut."

DB haiku "Valentine to My Sweet Away," on Carl Smool 4-color silkscreen poster for 2/14/79 *Origin of the Valentine* DB reading at Book Project, Seattle—198 copies, 20 deluxe signed by artist, by poet, kissed with red lipstick by 19-year-old Gail Stavdal, who is portrayed on poster.

DB poem "A Self Portrait," [+ poems by Creseyde, Lee, Charlin, Michael from DB's *Miracle Finger: A Book of Works by Children*], Floating Poetry Gallery, a traveling exhibition through Seattle government buildings, conceived and curated by Kerry Ruef, opening at Greenwood Gallery, July 12, 1979. [DB read poem at 9/2/79 Bumbershoot, Floating Poetry Gallery reading.]

DB poem "Song," one of six chosen in the original national competition for display in Pittsburgh, Atlanta, Detroit, Denver, Los Angeles, 15 other cities across USA, *Poetry on the Buses*, Carnegie-Mellon University, the Department of Transportation, National Endowment for the Arts, Pennsylvania Council on the Arts, "Poet Dick Bakken, artist Gage Taylor, Designer Eddie Byrd," 1979.

"In the Sanctuary of Our Sorrowful Mother" [re-titled with the poem origin site for this use, DB's "This Morning"], ed. by Steven Nemerow, Stephen Thomas, Barbara la Morticella, *Confluence: A Portland Anthology*, limited ed.

150 letterpress copies, 1979, with enlarged-page gallery exhibition, Multnomah Art Center, Portland, Oregon.

Grace, textile serigraph monoprint, DB poem over various tie-dyed napalm-explosion colors silkscreened onto torn rectangles of bed sheet, Carl Smool Rag Series #1, 1988, 20 copies, **o.p.**

DB poem "Grace," one of six winners, displayed in 8' × 16', Bumbershoot Big Book exhibition, Small Press Bookfair, *Bumbershoot: Seattle Arts Festival*, 1988, curated by director Judith Roche.

DB poem "Priest of the Bees," displayed in 4' × 10', Bumbershoot Big Book exhibition, Small Press Bookfair, *Bumbershoot: Seattle Arts Festival*, 1990, curated by director Judith Roche.

"World Hunger Etiquette," DB poem in five parts composed or improvised through exercises commonly used with children—a text commissioned by the Scottsdale Cultural Council to be performed in response to and in front of *Escoffier* (1982), a welded curtain of over a thousand dinner knives, by Arman (b. France, 1928), *The International Art Show for the End of World Hunger*, Scottsdale Center for the Arts, Arizona, January 10, 1990, art show traveling globally.

DB poem "The Names" with slides of names, some from *Egon Schiele: Sketchbooks* in "Word Becomes Art: a brief exploration of a long-standing relationship, a performance edited by Karen Bowden and Ron Dickson for the Scottsdale Center for the Arts," Scottsdale, Arizona, 1992.

DB poems "Tamarack," "Twilight," *Poetry in the Environment*, Tucson Poetry Festival, Arizona, 1992, poems placed around town during festival week, similar to menu tents on restaurant tables.

DB poems in handsewn, letterpress, limited editions, "Tree," "Grace," "Going into Moonlight," *Thirty Years of Contemporary Poetry: Artifacts, Images, Cultures*, University of Arizona Poetry Center 30th anniversary celebration, traveling exhibition, a month at each: Tucson/Pima Public Library (April 2–30, 1992), Rincon/University High School Library (May 1–22, 1992), Nogales/Santa Cruz County Public Library (June 1–27, 1992), City of Sierra Vista Community Center (July 1–31, 1992), Copper Queen Public Library, Bisbee (August 3–29, 1992), Casa Grande Public Library (September 1–30, 1992), Tucson High Magnet School (October 5–30, 1992), Yuma County Library District, Main Library (November 2–28, 1992), Green Valley Recreation Center (December 1–31, 1992), Phoenix Central Library (January 4–30, 1993). Preview,

Tucson Poetry Festival X, historic Studio "Y," March 6–8, 1992. At Bisbee Poetry Festival, August 7–9, 1992.

Ruth Bush, poster [old-time movies design] with watercolor of DB and dancer Caryl Clement, "Monsoon! / Bisbee Poetry Festival 1992 / A Downpour of Poetry, Painting, Dance, Foreign Language, Physics & Video." DB owns original framed artwork, purchased from Bush for $100.

DB poem recommended by Naomi Shihab Nye to curator, who said Nye used it in her classes all the time to teach making something from simplicity, "How to Eat Corn," as enlarged calligraphy display for *Exhibition on Corn*, curator Zet Baer, San Antonio Children's Museum, Texas, 1996.

Flight, painter Sally Brock, poet Dick Bakken, Twist Gallery of Contemporary Art, exhibition and performance, Bisbee, Arizona, opening May 27, 2005, collector's poster by artist John Annesley.

DB poem "Grace," artist Ed Lee piece expressing DB poem, *Children's Memorial*, a traveling exhibition curated by Dale Clark, opening in Tombstone, Arizona, then Bisbee, Tucson, 2005.

DB poem "Grace," *100 American Poets Against the War*, Metropolitan Arts Press, Chicago, with publication and exhibition, The Chicago Athenaeum Museum of Architecture and Design, 2005.

Vehichulart, photographer John Annesley, poet Dick Bakken, cellist Joanna Emmott, exhibition and closing performance, Market Street Coffee Co. at DC Ranch, Scottsdale, Arizona, 2/25/06.

DB's "The Huge High Engines Unheard," "Nicaragua," *War!* an art & poetry exhibition curated by poet Leslie Clark, Student Union Gallery, Cochise College, Douglas, Arizona, opening with an October 25, 2005, reading by DB and the other poets.

Stefanie Marlis poem, "May You Never Know What Lies Ahead," her annual Christmas card, in letterpress by Richard Serbert, design by Sharrie Brooks, limited edition, 300 copies, of a poem based on DB real life events, 1999.

Designed by DB, *Deport Poets* black T-shirts with white-slash paint-like lettering, as if graffiti on sides of 1917 boxcars hauling Wobblies away, silkscreen printings 1981, and years following, hundreds sold at Bisbee Poetry Festivals and carried on book tours, now worn by so many poets.

Poetry Books from *Pleasure Boat Studio: A Literary Press*

Listed chronologically by release date. **Note: Empty Bowl Press** is a Division of Pleasure Boat Studio.

For My Father ~ Amira Thoron ~ $17
Return to a Place Like Seeing ~ John Palmer ~ $17
Ascendance ~ Tim McNulty ~ $16
Alter Mundus ~ Lucia Gizzino ~ trans. from Italian by Michael Daley ~ $15.95
The Every Day ~ Sarah Plimpton ~ $15.95
A Taste ~ Morty Schiff ~ $15.95
Hanoi Rhapsodies ~ Scott Ezell ~ $10 ~ **an empty bowl book**
Dark Square ~ Peter Marcus ~ $14.95
Notes from Disappearing Lake ~ Robert Sund ~ $15
Taos Mountain ~ Paintings and poetry ~ Robert Sund ~ $45 (hardback only)
P'u Ming's Oxherding Pictures & Verses ~ trans. from Chinese by Red Pine ~ $15 ~
     an empty bowl book
Swimming the Colorado ~ Denise Banker ~ $16 ~ **an empty bowl book**
A Path to the Sea ~ Liliana Ursu, trans. from Romanian by Adam J. Sorkin and
     Tess Gallagher ~ $15.95
Songs from a Yahi Bow: Poems about Ishi ~ Yusef Komanyakaa, Mike O'Connor, Scott Ezell
     ~ $13.95
Beautiful Passing Lives ~ Edward Harkness ~ $15
Immortality ~ Mike O'Connor ~ $16
Painting Brooklyn ~ Paintings by Nina Talbot, Poetry by Esther Cohen ~ $20
Ghost Farm ~ Pamela Stewart ~ $13
Unknown Places ~ Peter Kantor, trans. from Hungarian by Michael Blumenthal ~ $14
Moonlight in the Redemptive Forest ~ Michael Daley ~ includes a CD ~ $16
Lessons Learned ~ Finn Wilcox ~ $10 ~ **an empty bowl book**
Jew's Harp ~ Walter Hess ~ $14
The Light on Our Faces ~ Lee Whitman-Raymond ~ $13
Petroglyph Americana ~ Scott Ezell ~ $15 ~ **an empty bowl book**
God Is a Tree, and Other Middle-Age Prayers ~ Esther Cohen ~ $10
Home & Away: The Old Town Poems ~ Kevin Miller ~ $15
Old Tale Road ~ Andrew Schelling ~ $15 ~ **an empty bowl book**
Working the Woods, Working the Sea ~ Eds. Finn Wilcox, Jerry Gorsline ~ $22 ~ **an empty
     bowl book**
The Blossoms Are Ghosts at the Wedding ~ Tom Jay ~ with essays ~ $15 ~ **an empty bowl book**
Against Romance ~ Michael Blumenthal ~ $14
Days We Would Rather Know ~ Michael Blumenthal ~ $14
Craving Water ~ Mary Lou Sanelli ~ $15
When the Tiger Weeps ~ Mike O'Connor ~ with prose ~ 15
Concentricity ~ Sheila E. Murphy ~ $13.95
The Immigrant's Table ~ Mary Lou Sanelli ~ with recipes ~ $14
Women in the Garden ~ Mary Lou Sanelli ~ $14
Saying the Necessary ~ Edward Harkness ~ $14
Nature Lovers ~ Charles Potts ~ $10
The Politics of My Heart ~ William Slaughter ~ $13
The Rape Poems ~ Frances Driscoll ~ $13

Desire ~ Jody Aliesan ~ $14 ~ **an empty bowl book**

Dreams of the Hand ~ Susan Goldwitz ~ $14 ~ **an empty bowl book**

The Basin: Poems from a Chinese Province ~ Mike O'Connor ~ $10 / $20 ~ **an empty bowl book** (paper/ hardbound)

The Straits ~ Michael Daley ~ $10 ~ **an empty bowl book**

In Our Hearts and Minds: The Northwest and Central America ~ Ed. Michael Daley ~ $12 ~ with prose ~ **an empty bowl book**

The Rainshadow ~ Mike O'Connor ~ $16 ~ **an empty bowl book**

Untold Stories ~ William Slaughter ~ $10 / $20 ~ **an empty bowl book** (paper / hardbound)

Our Chapbook Series:

No. 1: *The Handful of Seeds: Three and a Half Essays* ~ Andrew Schelling ~ $7 ~ nonfiction

No. 2: *Original Sin* ~ Michael Daley ~ $8

No. 3: *Too Small to Hold You* ~ Kate Reavey ~ $8

No. 4: *The Light on Our Faces*—re-issued in non-chapbook (see previous list)

No. 5: *Eye* ~ William Bridges ~ $8

No. 6: *Selected* **New Poems** *of Rainer Maria Rilke* ~ trans. fm German by Alice Derry ~ $10

No. 7: *Through High Still Air: A Season at Sourdough Mountain* ~ Tim McNulty ~ $9 ~ with prose

No. 8: *Sight Progress* ~ Zhang Er, trans. fm Chinese by Rachel Levitsky ~ $9 ~ prosepoems

No. 9: *The Perfect Hour* ~ Blas Falconer ~ $9

No. 10: *Fervor* ~ Zaedryn Meade ~ $10

No. 11: *Some Ducks* ~ Tim McNulty ~ $10

No. 12: *Late August* ~ Barbara Brackney ~ $10

No. 13: *The Right to Live Poetically* ~ Emily Haines ~ $9

From other publishers (in limited editions):

In Blue Mountain Dusk ~ Tim McNulty ~ $12.95 ~ a Broken Moon Press book

China Basin ~ Clemens Starck ~ $13.95 ~ a Story Line Press book

Journeyman's Wages ~ Clemens Starck ~ $10.95 ~ a Story Line Press book

Orders: Pleasure Boat Studio books are available by order from your bookstore, directly from our website, or through the following:

SPD (Small Press Distribution) Tel. 800-869-7553, Fax 510-524-0852

Partners/West Tel. 425-227-8486, Fax 425-204-2448

Baker & Taylor Tel. 800-775-1100, Fax 800-775-7480

Ingram Tel. 615-793-5000, Fax 615-287-5429

Amazon.com or **Barnesandnoble.com**

Pleasure Boat Studio: A Literary Press
201 West 89th Street
New York, NY 10024
Fax: 413-677-0085
www.pleasureboatstudio.com / pleasboat@nyc.rr.com

CPSIA information can be obtained
at www.ICGtesting.com
Printed in the USA
FFOW02n0028180814
6827FF